THE NEW CEO

THE New CEO

THE NEW CEO

GEORGE A. STEINER

Harry and Elsa Kunin
Professor of Business and Society
and
Professor of Management
University of California, Los Angeles

Studies of the Modern Corporation
Graduate School of Business
Columbia University

MACMILLAN PUBLISHING CO., INC.
NEW YORK

COLLIER MACMILLAN PUBLISHERS
LONDON

Macmillan Publishing Co., Inc.
866 Third Avenue, New York, N.Y. 10022

Collier Macmillan Canada, Inc.

Library of Congress Catalog Card Number: 82–48599

Printed in the United States of America

printing number

1   2   3   4   5   6   7   8   9   10

Library of Congress Cataloging in Publication Data

Steiner, George Albert
  The new CEO.

  (Studies of the modern corporation)
  Includes index.
  1. Executives—United States.   I. Title.
II. Title: CEO.   III. Series.
HF5500.3.U54S746   1983   658.4'00973   82–48599
ISBN 0–02–931250–7

STUDIES OF THE MODERN CORPORATION
Graduate School of Business, Columbia University

The Program for Studies of the Modern Corporation is devoted to the advancement and dissemination of knowledge about the corporation. Its publications are designed to stimulate inquiry, research, criticism, and reflection. They fall into three categories: works by outstanding businesspeople, scholars, and professionals from a variety of backgrounds and academic disciplines; annotated and edited selections of business literature; and business classics that merit republication. The studies are supported by outside grants from private business, professional, and philanthropic institutions interested in the program's objectives.

RICHARD EELLS
Director

Contents

Contents

Contents

Preface

E<small>VERYONE</small> knows that the social and political environment of business is changing. Not everyone fully appreciates, however, the extent to which these changes are affecting business. The forces that are influencing the environment of business—and thereby the internal functioning of business—are powerful, fundamental, numerous, and generally threatening.

This book summarizes the results of my research into the ways in which external forces are changing the management task of the chief executive officers (CEOs) of our largest corporations. I conclude that these CEOs are spending an increasing amount of their time on problems stemming from external factors, that collectively they have changed their basic strategies that deal with social and political forces in the environment, and that they believe the requirements for a person to be an effective CEO (today and in the future) are far broader than in the past. Indeed, so different are these qualities from those thought important in the past that it is not any exaggeration to speak of "the new CEO." This new CEO is well represented in the sample of CEOs on which this study was based.

Early in this study it became clear that the changes being made in the managerial task of the CEO were also altering the internal organizational structure of the corporation, relationships of the CEO with the board of directors and with line managers and staff, as well as the function of different groups within the corporate organization. This book is an examination of some of the major recent developments in these aspects of our large corporations.

It is an hypothesis of this study that, for our large corporations particularly, the model of the new breed of CEO as outlined here is one that will be followed in general terms by more and more business executives in the future. It is not expected that the adoption of the model will be rapid and widespread but rather that it will be slow and steady.

The phrase "Chief Executive Officer" and its abbreviation "CEO" when used in this book refers, of course, to the person in a company who carries that title. But in some companies there is no one with the title of "Chief Executive Officer," and, in such instances, "CEO" refers to the top executive in the company irrespective of his or her title.

The sample of CEOs and other executives on which this study was based is admittedly highly selective. As shown in the Appendix, forty-seven executives, including twenty-five CEOs, in the largest companies in the United States were interviewed. It certainly cannot be said that CEOs in much smaller corporations face either the problems of the CEOs of the larger corporations or have responded in the same way to external forces as their peers in the largest companies. However, the example of how the social and political environment is influencing the large corporation represented in this study is more likely than not to be felt by an increasing number of companies in the future.

This report is based on several dozens of interviews with executives, many speeches and reports of CEOs of large corporations, and my own observation and study of the corporation over many years. In this report I have supported my observations with extensive quotations from others, especially CEOs.

The words that are quoted are taken at face value. No effort is made to evaluate and analyze them. It is my belief that virtually all the executives surveyed for this study will, except in a few places, which are noted, accept its basic conclusions. However, I am sure that among them there will be different interpretations of the words and ideas expressed here.

For those readers who are critical of various business practices, I should say that no one, including the executives represented in this report, denies that there are many of these that should be corrected. But the purpose of this study is not to examine them.

On the other hand, the results of this study show, in the CEOs participating in it, I believe, a remarkable degree of enlightenment, a commitment to manage in the public—as well as in the private—interest, a surprising forbearance of unenlightened government regulations, an intent to respond appropriately to all legitimate interests focused on the business corporation, and a balanced understanding of the changing role of business in society.

When speaking of the totality of forces that affect the managerial task of top executives in our large corporations, I mean those forces inside as well as outside the company. Internal forces affecting the management task, to illustrate, would include changing attitudes of people towards authority, the changing work ethic, and the demands of managers for greater participation in the decision processes. The external forces include government regulations, economic conditions, expectations of company constituents, attitudes of environmental groups, the legal system, and so on.

For readers of this book who may not have a clear perception of these forces, I have devoted Chapter 1 to a succinct description of the types of changing forces that affect business, externally and internally. Readers who are knowledgeable about these forces, should, of course, move rapidly over Chapter 1 or skip it completely.

Many people contributed to this study. I wish here to thank them, especially the executives whom I was privileged to interview. Their names are listed in the Appendix. Many people read all or part of this book. I am grateful to each of them for their comments even though I did not always follow their advice and counsel. I am happy to extend special thanks to Chauncey G. Olinger, Jr., for his skillful editing of the manuscript for this book.

It is my hope that this book will lead to a better understanding of the managerial tasks of the top executives of our large corporations, and of the skills and attitudes that are needed—and are being employed by these executives and their staffs—in discharging these tasks. It is my hope that the exemplary model presented in this book will be adopted by more boards of directors of our business institutions when they face the question of choosing a new CEO for their company. An increased use of this model seems to me to be especially important because I believe the preservation of the best of our business institutions will depend in no small degree upon it. Finally, I hope this book will motivate and in some degree point the way to improved curricula in our schools of business/management/administration. I hope curricula will be developed to reflect the ways in which the changing external environment of business is altering the management task and the internal business infrastructure. I also hope curricula will be developed to improve the training of managers to meet the requirements suggested by the model of the new CEOs set forth in this book.

GEORGE A. STEINER
Los Angeles
November 1982

THE NEW CEO

1

Changes in the Environment of Business That Challenge the CEO

THERE is no doubt at all that the social and political environment of business has changed dramatically during the past ten to fifteen years. It is important to understand the major dimensions of this change in order to appreciate the new developments that have taken place in the management task of the CEO of the large corporation and in the internal structure and decision-making processes of these corporations.

External forces influencing business are vast in number and scope. We do not try here to provide an extended analysis of them, but rather to give brief sketches of the major changes that are shaping today's business environment.[1]

The Recent Adoption of Non-Traditional Values

Highly important in the current turbulence of the environment of business are changes in the values that people hold. In recent years, the increasing adoption of values that have not previously played a major role in American society have stimulated new massive government regulations of business, deep criticisms of business, new demands on business, and challenges to the traditional fundamental values on which the business institution has rested. For example, more and more people arc less and less willing to accept the impartial operation of free market mechanisms as the best way to allocate resources. As a result they turn more and more to government to intervene in their behalf.

Expanded versions of equalitarianism are challenging older distributive principles. Traditionally, equality meant that conditions should permit individuals, whatever their origins, to make a life on the basis of ability and character. It was the idea that everyone should have an equal place at "the starting line." In recent years, the concept of equality has broadened to include rights to receive a wide range of political, social, and economic benefits. Daniel Bell, Professor of Sociology, Harvard University, has called this "The Revolution of Rising Entitlements."[2] More recently this concept has turned into one of equality of results, or an equal outcome for all. John Rawls, Professor of Philosophy, Harvard University, a central proponent of the new equalitarianism, argues that people are born with different natural abilities and are raised under different circumstances. As a result, not everyone approaches the starting line equally. In this light, he argues, fairness and justice necessitate equalization of results.[3] This value, according to *Business Week* in 1975, is "the greatest single force changing and expanding the role of the federal government in the U.S. today."[4]

There are many other value changes that directly or indirectly influence business.[5] People today insist on economic security—even fulfillment—now rather than later. They want the good things of life early in their careers and have steadily rising expectations. They want to experience a continuously improved quality of life.[6] There is a growing challenge of, and cynicism towards, authority and an erosion of that part of the Protestant Ethic that motivates people to high standards of work performance. People want a more comfortable and less risky life. They are no longer willing to accept the traditional legal rights of property ownership but wish society to influence the way property is used. Profit is no longer universally accepted as the goal of business. Society is coming more and more to expect that its interests be considered as well as those of business in the pursuit of profit objectives, especially in the large corporation. Some observers see in such trends a serious erosion of the fundamental institutional values that underlie the classical free enterprise system.[7]

New Demands on Business

Forces such as these create new demands on business. The Committee for Economic Development, a group of prominent people in business, described the demands and the challenge to business in this way:

> Today it is clear that the terms of the contract between society and business are, in fact, changing in substantial and important ways. Business is being asked to assume broader responsibilities to society than ever before and to serve a wider range of human values. Business enterprises, in effect, are being asked to contribute more to the quality of American life than just supplying quantities of goods and services. Inasmuch as business exists to serve society, its future will depend on the quality of management's responses to the changing expectations of the public.[8]

The broad demand for an improved quality of life has been translated into specific public cries for everything from a pollution-free environment to improved quality in products. The range of demands touches virtually every facet of the operation of businesses both large and small. These demands do not supplant the traditional economic obligations of business; rather, they are an addition to the traditional responsibility of business firms to use scarce resources efficiently in producing goods and services that people want at prices they are willing to pay. Unfortunately, society has not yet spelled out in much detail how these two responsibilities are to be met.

In pursuit of its political and economic goals, the Reagan Administration has reduced federal social expenditures and, at this writing, is asking the Congress to reduce such expenditures further. At the same time, the President is asking the private sector to increase its commitment of time and money to social programs. Community pressure on corporations can also be expected to grow along with cuts in federal social programs.

Criticisms of Business

Opinion polls show that Americans are highly critical of all their institutions, but the business institution, especially the large corporation, has elicited special criticisms. Public respect for business has declined drastically during the past decade and is today at a very low level.[9] Such antipathy toward business has its roots far back in history.[10] And certainly throughout U.S. history the average person has had a deep distrust of large organizations. In many respects business has not changed, but attitudes towards it, new standards of behavior, and excessive expectations have inflamed people against business.

The American public is specific about its criticisms of business, as the opinion polls reveal. For instance, 43 percent believe that big companies can get away with just about anything, legal or otherwise; 61 percent think the most important causes of inflation are excess profits; 67 percent are of the opinion that most companies twist the facts in advertising and don't tell the truth; 56 percent believe consumers do not get a "fair shake"; and 70 percent think government is run by a few big interests looking out for themselves.[11] Business is also criticized for making shoddy products, charging excessive prices, depressing wage rates, and on and on.

Despite these sharp criticisms of business and the change in values by which people judge the business institution (noted above), there is strong support for the type of private enterprise system now existing in the United States. A poll by Daniel Yankelovich, corroborated by others, reveals that 60 percent of the population say they would sacrifice if necessary to preserve the free enterprise system.[12] In a national survey of American professors, 81 percent agreed that "the private business system in the U.S., for all its flaws, works better than any other system devised for advanced industrial society."[13]

Such opinions strongly support the free enterprise institution, despite some differences in the way people define it. If the underlying institution is not in question, where is the critical focus on business? It lies, Yankelovich has said, in serious complaints about the way in which business is operated: the treatment of consumers, pollution of the atmosphere by businesses, the alleged exercise of business power contrary to the public interest, and so on. Yet, he continued, there is a vast reservoir of respect in the nation for the efficiency of business and its problem-solving capabilities.[14]

A more serious problem exists, Yankelovich said, with respect to popular perceptions of the moral quality of business conduct. The average person has a deep mistrust of the motives of people in business. There is a strong belief that business people are primarily concerned with their own self-interests rather than the interests of those they serve, and that they frequently act immorally. People generally accept the idea that business must earn profits, but they believe business immorally extracts excessive profits.[15] Despite the fact that these perceptions of profiteering are highly distorted, they nonetheless persist.

Attitudes such as these accentuate and accelerate government regulation of business. They lead to punitive forms of regulation, which are costly and disruptive to business and adversely affect economic-political balances. Criticism of business, when justified, can be effective in improving its performance; when it is distorted, ill-founded, and excessive, however, it can easily lead to excessive government regulation.

Government Regulations

There is today practically no aspect of business that governments cannot—and will not—regulate if the occasion arises to do so and popular or legislative support exists for it. In recent years, governments have responded affirmatively to a wide range of public concerns about such matters as product safety, product labeling, pollution, minority employment, consumer risks, advertising, honesty, working safety, and pension systems. Accordingly, laws have been passed to deal with such concerns. The new regulations, especially those of the federal government, have resulted in an extraordinary new body of regulation. When added to all that was enacted previously, the mountain of regulation is truly staggering.

By far the most important concerns of the executives surveyed in this report relate to government regulation. This is not difficult to understand when one considers the variety and complexity of the powerful government forces that affect decision-making in business. Some of the major aspects of this flood of regulation are:

The Volume of Government Regulations

It is not easy to portray in a few words the sheer volume of regulations to which business is subject. As late as the mid-1950s, the federal government had assumed major regulatory responsibility in only four areas: antitrust, financial institutions, transportation, and communications. In 1970, eighty-three important federal agencies were involved in regulating private business activity. Of these, thirty-four had been created after 1960.[16] Another dimension is the passage of major pieces of legislation. To illustrate, in the 1970s, the Congress passed forty-two major pieces of legislation concerning environmental and resource conservation.[17]

The effect of government regulations varies among industries and companies. A small company in financial trouble may easily be pushed into bankruptcy by a comparatively minor regulation that a large, financially secure company will not notice as a cost consideration. But no company today fails to feel a substantial burden from the totality of government regulations. To illustrate, the National Council on Wage and Price Stability made a study concerning the impact of regulations on the steel industry. It listed 5,600 regulations from 27 agencies with which steelmakers must comply. These regulations ranged from very costly antipollution standards to one that required that workers wash their hands and faces before eating lunch.[18]

The present volume of government regulations of business is so large that no corporation can faithfully comply with all the laws and regulations to which it is subject. Commenting on this point Walter Wriston, the CEO of Citibank, said:

> What worries me is that General Motors and Citibank have a fighting chance of obeying all the new regulatory laws because we have the staff and the big-time lawyers to do so. But most small business people do not. They cannot even find out what the law is. There are, for example, 1,200 interpretations by the Federal Reserve staff of the Truth in Lending Act. Now 90% of the more than 14,000 commercial banks in this country have fewer than 100 employees. If you gave every staff member those regulations and started them reading, they wouldn't be finished by next year.[19]

The Growing Costs of Regulation

The cost of complying with federal regulations, not to mention state and local laws, is very significant and rising rapidly. It is not easy to calculate the costs of regulation but a few numbers give some idea of the dimensions. The Center for the Study of American Business, Washington University, St. Louis, calculates that in fiscal 1979 the aggregate cost of government regulation was about $102.7 billion.[20] The Council on Environmental Quality estimates that the costs of complying with environmental regulations will be $477.6 billion (in 1978 dollars), in addition to expenditures that would normally be made, in the period 1978–87.[21] General Motors Corporation calculates that in calendar year 1979 it employed 26,000 people just to comply with government regulations.[22] A study of the direct incremental costs incurred by forty-eight companies in complying with the regulations of only six federal agencies in 1977 amounted to 16 percent of their after-tax income.[23]

One should not overlook federal government data requirements when considering the costs of regulations. Recently, the Federal Paperwork Commission estimated that the total cost of federal paperwork to the entire nation was around $100 billion a year. The amount borne by private industry was calculated by the Commission to be between $25 and $32 billion a year. The ten thousand largest firms in the United States were estimated to spend from $10 to $12 billion a year on regulatory matters, or around $1 million per year each.[24]

There are offsetting benefits of government regulations, which will be discussed later, but there are also many illustrations of the costs of regulations exceeding benefits. Thus, Irving S. Shapiro, the former Chairman of the Board of du Pont, said that his company spent $1.2 million to reduce particulate emissions from one of its plants by 94 percent. He said that he believed that this expenditure was justified. The federal regulators, however, decided that emissions should be reduced an additional 3 percent. The cost to do this, said Shapiro, was $1.8 million and it resulted in no detectable difference in air quality. This expenditure, he said, was equivalent to paying 80 cents for a dozen eggs and an additional $1.20 for a piece of eggshell.[25]

Older and More Recent Regulations

Older federal regulations of business were characterized by controls over specific industries, such as the railroads (Interstate Commerce Commission—ICC), airlines (Civilian Aviation Board —CAB), and drugs(Food and Drug Administration—FDA).Newer regulations, by contrast, are concerned with one business function and cut across industrial lines. Some important implications flow from this difference. One is that the newer agencies can profoundly influence a company's affairs in one functional area and do so with a limited understanding and concern for the effect on the total operations of the company.[26] Another consequence is the tendency of the newer agencies, both by legislative mandate and executive inclination, to become intimately involved in managerial decision-making. The case of automobile manufacturers is in point. Government directly influences management decisions about automobile designs, pricing, advertising, research and development, warranties, production methods, recalls, and technology.

The older regulatory agencies were designed to prevent monopoly and improve competition in the marketplace. The newer agencies, on the other hand, that regulate business, such as the Environmental Protection Agency (EPA), the Equal Employment Opportunity Commission (EEOC), the Consumer Product Safety Commission (CPSC), and the Occupational Safety and Health Administration (OSHA), have a variety of purposes and apply different policies and methods to regulation. Newer regulations are the results of pressures to improve the quality of life. In discharging their responsibilities, the newer agencies usually exercise a "command and control" method of regulation in contrast to the method of using incentives to influence decision-making in the marketplace. The latter type of control provides an opportunity for corporate managers to choose from alternatives in meeting regulatory objectives that the command and control technique denies.[27]

Nonsense, Trivia, and Conflict among Regulations

Newer regulations, particularly early ones of OSHA, are replete with nonsense and trivia, such as "Jacks which are out of order shall be tagged accordingly, and shall not be used until repairs are made."[28] As another example, Armco Steel reports that the cost of paperwork in connection with a $10 license payment for heavy trucks at one of its plants was $1,240. The company's request to pay a $25 fee in lieu of supplying this information was turned down.[29]

As the details of regulations penetrate more deeply into business operations the conflicts among them mount. They involve broad contradictions such as EPA pollution controls, which add costs to products and partly negate federal anti-inflation policies. A recent suit of Sears, Roebuck & Company sets forth in great detail many specific conflicts among federal regulations concerning minorities in the workplace that complicate—if not prevent—a corporation's full compliance with the regulations.[30]

8

A very significant conflict has arisen due to the shift that has taken place from market to political-legal decisions. Unfortunately, what is politically rational is often economically irrational, and vice versa. As government interferes more and more in the market-place, it follows that more and more economic irrationality is injected into the nation's economic life.

New Technical Issues Raised by Regulations

The new regulations raise (as well as reflect) significant and controversial technological issues. For instance, there are extremely sensitive issues that have arisen with respect to equating statistical measures of the loss of life with costs of controls. For example, one study concluded that FDA regulations unduly delay the introduction of new drugs on the market so that fewer lives are saved by them than should be possible.[31] Of course, different lives are involved. How should the cost-benefit equation be balanced?

No one really knows how much of a given chemical particulate or gas in the atmosphere may cause some illness, to someone, at some time. Yet, regulations are proposed and/or announced that create difficult and costly problems of compliance. Unfortunately, there are wide differences of opinion about the need for, and the results of, much of this regulation. For instance, the Delaney Cancer Amendment of 1958 to the Miller Act of 1954, which was an amendment to the Food, Drug, and Cosmetic Act of 1938, allows the FDA no leeway whatever in prohibiting the addition to food of any substance known to produce cancer in any species, in any dosage, and under any circumstances. On the basis of this amendment the Secretary of the Department of Health, Education and Welfare has eliminated cyclamates and threatened to take saccharin from the market because laboratory tests have showed that they caused cancer in mice.

Both rulings were based on the results of feeding high dosages to laboratory animals. In the case of cyclamates, for instance, to get as much cyclamate as the rats, it would be necessary for a person to drink several cases of cyclamate-sweetened soft drinks every day for most of a normal life-span. This seems silly. Laboratory experimenters, however, claim that, silly or not, the tests do prove that the additive is carcinogenic to mice and, by inference, to human beings. Assuming this to be so, the question then be-

9

comes: What is the cost-benefit trade-off? In the case of saccharin, for example, one physicist concluded that "if all other things were unchanged, the substitution of diet for nondiet drinks would increase life expectancy by 100 times more than the cancer risk reduced it."[32] The Delaney amendment made some sense when all the carcinogens that were found in foods were potent and in high concentration. As we have become much more sophisticated in identifying and measuring carcinogens, modifications in the law must be made to provide for weak concentrations.

With growing scientific knowledge, more and more hazards to life are becoming apparent. Decisions about many technical matters, such as whether to put fluorocarbons or another substance in spray-propelled fluids, no longer are being left to private industry. But frequently no one knows in these cases what a rational decision is or how it should be made.

New biological, chemical, and other findings are continuously raising difficult technical questions. They reflect, of course, a growing awareness of the hazards to human life and the national policy to reduce them. The policy is not in question here, but the fact is that new regulations do become embroiled in controversial technical issues undreamed of in the past.

Administrative Decision-Making Delays

Delays in government regulatory decision-making are not new, but in recent years lengthy court hearings and slow agency decision-making have not only been costly to business but have inhibited initiative in the development of new technology. To cite a few illustrations, John W. Hanley, Chairman and President of Monsanto Company, said that his company's Roundup herbicide was developed in 1970 after fifteen years of research. It was not until 1975 that the product received approval from the federal government for use on major grain crops. It was not until three years later that approval was given for use on other crops. He added that: "The irony is that regulation has slowed the introduction of a pesticide that is environmentally more attractive than many of those now on the market."[33] In 1977, Dow Chemical U.S.A. abandoned plans for a multimillion-dollar petrochemical complex in Northern California because two years of effort and an expenditure of $4 million had gained the company only four approvals out of 65 required official permits.[34] A utility must get clearance from thirty agencies to build a plant in California, and any one of the agencies can deny the permit. A final illustration of the delays in government decision-making is the fact that the antitrust suit brought against IBM by the government was finally settled in January 1982 after eleven years.

Underlying Causes of Expanding Regulations

There are many reasons for the recent spate of new government regulations, and these must be understood if one is to have a balanced perspective about current regulatory patterns. Space does not permit extensive analysis of the forces for expansion, and so only a few significant ones are noted and briefly described.

First, in the 1960s there was a growing realization that, for the first time in history, this nation had solved "the economic problem," the problem of providing a minimum of goods and services to virtually every person in the population. People's attention then turned from production to improving the quality of life. This meant high and rising minimum income, greater equality of opportunity, better quality products at lower prices, a pollution-free atmosphere, more information for consumers, accountability for business, and so on. The thrust for such improvements resulted in government regulations to help achieve these new expectations because business simply could not meet them, many of which were far beyond reality.

Second, more concern for individuals has resulted in more legislation in their behalf. It is laudable for government to seek to assure such things as safer working conditions, better and safer products for consumers, the elimination of discrimination in employment. Recent efforts in this area do not represent a new departure for government, but rather an intensification of past policy.

Third, government has stepped in to meet society's needs when the market has failed. A classic illustration, of course, is pollution. One steel mill that tries to eliminate its air and water pollution will go bankrupt if others in the industry are not required to install antipollution equipment. The same principle applies to industrial safety practices and health hazards.

Fourth, demands to prevent alleged or visible business abuses are often described in the media. The Equity Funding scandal is a good illustration.

Fifth, the population is becoming better educated and tends to

11

be knowledgeable, cynical, and critical. It is increasingly disposed to seek from government redress from proven or imagined grievances.

Sixth, regulations are adopted to achieve other social goals such as national security, allocation of scarce resources, provision of services to small communities, and the redistribution of income.

All these underlying reasons for expanding government regulations are understandable and acceptable. The issue today is not the justification for a particular type of regulation, but the choice of regulatory methods and the sheer volume and cost of the regulations.

An Overall Cost/Benefit Evaluation

This evaluation by no means exhausts the roster of the results of government regulation of business, although it does highlight some of the more serious negative effects, which raise questions about the cost/benefit equation of government regulation. On the benefit side it must be observed that regulations have protected and subsidized business interests as well as consumer and general public interests. Regulations have helped society to achieve generally accepted economic and social goals. They have helped to improve the position of minorities, achieve cleaner air, reduce physical maladies associated with pollution, prevent abuses of the market mechanism, prevent monopolistic practices, and reduce industrial accidents. The list of advantages of government regulation is long and must not be underestimated.

On the other hand, there are substantial "costs" of today's government regulations, using "costs" in a broad sense. In the aggregate, the costs of today's government regulation seem greater than the benefits. Twenty-five years ago the power scale between business and government was balanced reasonably well.[35] Even twelve years ago the balance did not appear to this writer to be too uneven.[36] Today the overall balance is significantly upset in favor of government.

A badly skewed balance between government control and business freedom not only saps the effectiveness of business today but may, if continued, lead to socioeconomic disruption with more serious consequences. For instance, Harold M. Williams, the former Chairman of the Securities and Exchange Commission, has concluded that:

In the interests of equality and fairness, we are becoming so en-
meshed in regulation that we may hobble, rather than reshape, our
institutions—whether they be business, the community, or whatever.
Stated differently, while we permit the political process to impose
necessary egalitarianism on the market, there is no corresponding
mechanism which encourages the political process to consider the
impact of its actions on the economy.[37]

This suggests, of course, that increasing attention be given to
reforming the regulatory system.

Reforming Governmental Business Regulatory Systems

During the past half century there have been strong programs
to reform government regulatory systems. They have ranged from
prestigious Presidential and gubernatorial commissions to continuing high-priority policies and programs. Many of them did result
in important reforms, but collectively they did not reverse the major
governmental regulatory trends that were described above. The
Reagan Administration has given high priority to reforming the
federal regulatory system and has taken positive steps to eliminate
many regulations that were considered to be unwise, unjust, or
excessive in light of cost and potential benefit. The previous, Carter
Administration adopted and pursued the same policy without much
success. Whether the Reagan Administration's efforts will be more
successful in reforming the federal regulatory system remains to
be seen.[38] Even the most optimistic assessment of success for the
Reagan Administration's programs, however, will not spell more
than a marginal diminution of the massive pile of present-day
regulations of governments—federal, state, and local. Nor will federal regulatory reform blunt the major strong pressures in this
society for more rather than less government regulation of business. The best that can be hoped for is a slowing down of the trend
of growing government regulations and a reduction in specific
unwise, unjust, and unnecessary regulations.

It should also be noted that this Administration's "New Feder-
alism," which seeks to shift much federal government activity to
state and local governments, may exacerbate the governmental
regulatory problems of business. Instead of dealing with one agency
in Washington, D.C., a manager may find it necessary to deal with
many agencies throughout the nation concerned with a particular
governmental activity.

13

The Economic Environment

The economic environment covers a vast territory and is of central importance to business. It is a source of great opportunity as well as of serious danger. Indeed, the managerial task today is far more complex—and risky—than in the past in large part because of the rapid and puzzling changes taking place in the business economic environment to which a firm must adapt for its survival and profitable growth.

At this writing (November 1982), the economy of the United States, as well as that in other industrialized countries of the world, displays serious and alarming problems. The Gross National Product has registered an absolute decline and the consensus of forecasters is that economic recovery will not take place until well into 1983. While the rate of price inflation has dropped from double-digit levels to more moderate numbers, unemployment has risen nationally to 10 percent of the work force. Rates of unemployment in many areas are much higher. While interest rates have declined substantially in recent months, they are still at historically high levels. Our national productivity has fallen far below historical rates and is today less than that of any other major industrial nation of the world. Capital investment and research and development expenditures have dropped dramatically. A number of major industries are in truly depressed conditions—automobiles, construction, steel, for instance. Economic conditions in many cities and agricultural areas are very depressed. No one seems to have a clear idea about how the underlying economic forces in today's economy are likely to evolve in the future. There is no doubt about the fact, however, that these conditions create puzzling and major problems for everyone, including business managers.

In a different direction, society is increasing its demands that the ethical aspects of technical business decision-making be given greater recognition and attention. For instance, in the public mind it is becoming more ethically unacceptable to produce goods and services that pollute the atmosphere, that waste energy, or have built-in obsolescence features. Although such considerations may advance the public welfare, they do complicate the managerial decision-making processes.

In the international economic area, exporters of products and services as well as multinational corporations are encountering new and perplexing economic problems. They face a fluctuating value of the dollar in foreign exchange, powerful companies protected and partly subsidized by foreign governments, increasing competition from highly efficient foreign producers, and demands from host governments that they assume increased social and economic responsibilities as defined by those governments. Generally, their operations are being more and more restricted both by the government of the United States and of the countries in which they do business. And, it must not be overlooked that there are many areas of great social and political instability in the world, where the potential impacts on economic affairs raise grave questions of uncertainty and risk for American business.

On the other hand, of course, there are elements in the economic environment that provide great profit opportunities. The very size of the American market is itself a source of opportunity. Despite undulations above and below GNP trend lines, business activity in the past three decades has shown remarkably stable growth when compared with the prior decades. This stability has reduced substantially the type of uncertainties business faced in the unpredictable "boom and bust" cycles of the decades prior to World War II. New technologies are opening up opportunities for business. The fact that the world is not witnessing any wars of widespread destructiveness is a relatively stabilizing force for world business. New opportunities in government partnership with business, as in the areas of communications and energy, are opening up.

The Legal Environment

An executive of a large company remarked recently that ten years ago his principal legal worries centered on antitrust matters; everything else was lumped together as a poor second. But not today, he commented. Now, there are many areas of great legal urgency, the priorities of which change from month to month. As the number of problems have increased, attorney's fees and other legal costs have exploded. Indeed, he said that he now has set a goal of having annual earnings five times the legal fees of his company!

Thomas Ehrlich, Dean of the Law School at Stanford University, has used the phrase "legal pollution" to describe what he calls the growing feeling that it is virtually impossible to move "without running into a law or a regulation or a legal problem."[39] The new complex legal environment of business is due not only to increased government regulations but also to a new propensity in society to litigate. This trend is encouraged by the massive details of current laws, opportunities for different interpretations, and incentives to resist obeying the rules.

Not only are corporations subject to vastly expanded legal liabilities, but so are directors, officers, and other managers of business. Public demands are mounting that managers of corporations be held personally liable for illegal acts. The demands are not only for higher monetary levies for infractions of the law but jail sentences.[40] This trend is of concern to executives because new laws are often vague and it can take years to build the body of legal opinion that clarifies their meaning. Furthermore, well-financed "public interest" groups are an established part of the buisness environment these days and are ready to bring suit on slight provocation. In addition, the discovery of noncompliance with laws and regulations is much more likely today with the wide-ranging inspection rights of agencies like the Occupational Safety and Health Administration, the Internal Revenue Service, and the Securities and Exchange Commission. And as a result of Watergate and the foreign payoff scandals of recent years, the ethical character of corporate performance is high on the list of public concerns.

Finally, there are laws and statutes today that make managers guilty of a criminal act who have not themselves participated in that act. For instance, John R. Park, president of the multi-billion-dollar food chain Acme Markets, Inc., was personally held liable by the Supreme Court because he failed to ensure, as required by law, that his company kept rats out of a Baltimore warehouse.[41]

The Internal World of Business

Individuals within business organizations are demanding that their interests be considered in the managerial decision-making process. In the past, and within the law, businesses could make decisions wholly on the basis of economic factors. This is no longer possible. Individuals want more creative jobs; they want to participate in the business decision-making process; they want to avoid routine mind-numbing jobs; they want more pleasant surroundings; they want higher wages and more generous pensions; they want job security; and they want shorter hours and more vacations. Meeting such demands, within the competitive conditions facing most companies, is a difficult managerial task. But it is a challenge that managers of more and more companies accept. As Irving S. Shapiro, the recently retired CEO of du Pont, put it:

> The whole thrust of our society is toward greater individuality and better utilization of human potential. Our people are going to need a great deal of personal breadth and versatility. Our institutions are going to have to be flexible and offer a diversity of incentives and rewards. Our employee relations programs will have to take into account not just the job requirements as management sees them, but the plans and ambitions and preferences of individual employees as well. Finding the right fit between the goals of organizations and the goals of people working in them will be one of management's main tasks in the future.[42]

The Demands of a Pluralistic Society

Ours is a pluralistic society composed of autonomous and semi-autonomous groups through which power is diffused. A feature of our pluralism is that these groups are growing in total numbers, and there are many groups that have a deep antipathy towards business or espouse a point of view that is in sharp contrast to traditional business practices. There are also more and more groups armed with talented and dedicated members who understand how to use their power and existing laws to meet their objectives.

A fact of political life is the right of these groups to exert their influence in the seat of government. The decisions of government are frequently made in response to these pressures. Their influence on business is felt, therefore, through the legislative process. In addition, however, these groups are seeking to exercise more and more direct influence on business to act in their interests. In the distant past, a business manager could be successful if, working within the rules of the game laid down by government, he or she tried to satisfy only customers and stockholders. Today, the managers of a large corporation must pay attention to a growing number of constituent groups.[43] Dealing with the diverse, often conflicting, and sometimes disruptive pressures of such groups is consuming an increasing share of managerial time.

To make matters worse we are moving inexorably, Harold M. Williams said, "toward becoming a special interest society." He continued:

> Too many lobbyists and interest groups today either care absolutely nothing about the national interest as long as they get theirs or blithely assume that getting theirs is in the national interest. . . . The result has been an increasing polarization pitting those identified supporters of the "public interest" against backers of "private interest" as if the two were neatly and simply defined as opposed.[44]

Professor Bell looked at the same phenomenon and wrote: "The result is an increase in community conflict and in the politics of 'stymie'."[45]

It cannot be denied, of course, that business exerts power in the legislative and executive branches of government. But empirical observation makes quite clear the fact that business has lost power, relatively, in the political arena. David Vogel, Professor of Business Administration, University of California at Berkeley, pointed out:

> Between 1968 and 1977, the political influence of business was more than countervailed by a loosely allied but highly effective amalgam of consumer and environmental groups popularly referred to as "the public interest movement." Aided by a press that widely publicized numerous corporate abuses and inspired by the political, sophisticated leadership of spokesmen such as Ralph Nader, they were able to keep business on the defensive for nearly a decade.[46]

Other Environments of Business

There are many other important environments of business that affect the managerial job. For instance, there are the growingly inquisitive press and electronic media, which may publicize company activities objectively but which oftentimes, according to many managers, report the activities of companies distortedly if not erroneously. Managers find that they must pay careful attention to attitudes and perceptions of people in communities in which they operate. If not properly addressed, attitudes and perceptions about companies, their products and services, can create serious problems. Public utilities interested in constructing nuclear power plants illustrate the point well. The military environment is one of great significance to many companies. Changes in that environment can literally result in the life or death of companies involved in the military-industrial complex. Ideas in the intellectual community are watched carefully by many companies as portents of views that may become new demands on business. Many companies have discovered that changes in foreign policy of the United States can significantly affect their financial wellbeing.

Concluding Observations

No one can review this brief sketch of today's business environment without a sense that there has been a basic change in our society. Only a few years ago, the CEO of even a large company could spend most of his or her time on the nuts and bolts of the business. The focus was predominantly internal—how to improve efficiency to cut costs and reduce price while improving quality in order to be more competitive. The CEO's outward focus was essentially on the state of competition for the company products and services. Today, these affairs are still important but are matched and outranked in terms of top executive time and importance by many other environmental forces. We may well be in the midst of what cultural historians describe as an "axial age," or one of monumental transition. The scope of environmental concerns has enormously expanded for the CEO of the large company, and the priorities of attention have altered significantly within the past few years. The impact of these phenomena on the managerial task of the CEO of the large company has indeed been powerful.

2

CEO Time Allocated to External Forces

THERE is no question at all that CEOs today are spending far more time dealing with "external" issues than did their predecessors. Not only are they spending more time on such matters, but the nature of these forces that are of concern to them has altered dramatically, as we have noted in Chapter 1.

One of the questions the author asked CEOs concerned the amount of time they spent in their management tasks on external affairs in contrast to traditional (internal) economic and technical matters relating to the operation of their company. Recognizing, of course, the great difficulty in many instances of disentangling these two sets of concerns in the managerial task, we found the range of time spent on external matters was from 25 to 50 percent, on the average, with an occasional high of 80 or 90 percent. For instance, a company that is seeking to locate a plant in a particular place, or is trying to acquire other companies, or is involved in special problems with regulatory agencies may find its CEO spending most of his or her time on these matters over weeks or months.

These ranges agree with those found by other observers. Howard Chase, the editor of *Corporate Public Issues,* for instance, surveyed CEOs of the *Fortune* 1,000 companies on how much of their time they allocate to public issues that affect their company. In

1976, they said that such time averaged 20 percent, and, in 1978, it averaged about 40 percent.[1] Rogene Buchholz, then a professor at Washington University in St. Louis, surveyed CEOs on this point and found that the time spent on external matters by his sample ranged from 20 to 75 percent with a mode of 50 percent.[2] In 1969, the Conference Board surveyed CEOs and found only one among 127 who rated contact with the community and especially with government as being of most importance in the CEO's tasks.[3] Top priorities were given to planning, people, inspection, and control. This does not mean, of course, that executives in 1969 did not spend time on external affairs. They did, but generally not much, and external affairs were not rated as being of the highest priority to the CEOs of that day.

Many of the CEOs in our study said that ten to fifteen, and certainly twenty, years ago their predecessors spent very little if any time on external affairs, a marked contrast to today's practice. For example, Paul A. Miller, CEO of Pacific Lighting Corporation, said: "Ten years ago, I spent perhaps 15 percent of my time on matters related to regulation and/or governmental or public attitudes related to gas service." Mr. Miller added: "Today, that figure is well over 50 percent."[4]

The list of priorities for CEO attention has changed significantly over the past ten to fifteen years and varies, of course, from CEO to CEO and time to time. In the past, one or another aspect of the company's competitive position was high on the list of priorities for CEO attention. Today, the same matter may be far down on the list. For some, the changing attitudes of employees may be preeminent. For others, first place may be given to changing the values by which people judge business. For the CEO of a public utility, working with the Public Utility Commission may take precedence, while other public utility CEOs may find "environmentalists" most important. For the majority of CEOs of large companies, however, government would rank very high on the list if not first.

Government as a Priority for Attention

One major area of CEO concern is government regulation of the activities of their company. From the very inception of this nation governments have regulated business. In no previous period of our history, however, have government regulations been of more concern nor taken more of the time of CEOs than today. This is due to three strong forces. First is the accumulation of regulations over a long period of time. Throughout this century, particularly, the federal government, as well as state and local governments, have expanded the regulation of all sorts of business activities: competition, pricing, advertising, and so on. Under the New Deal of Franklin D. Roosevelt, the federal government undertook to correct a wide range of perceived abuses in the economic machinery of the nation, particularly in business, and amassed more far-reaching laws to this end in a shorter period of time than ever before or since. However, during the 1960s, especially, but also during the 1970s, a wide range of new laws were passed aimed at improving the quality of life. These laws were added to previous regulations to accumulate, as noted in Chapter 1, an unprecedented total volume of laws demanding business compliance.

Second, more and more regulations are directed at the important functional areas of business: production, employment, product quality, research and development, insurance and retirement, pricing, advertising, waste disposal, and so on. These regulations raise a growing number of major questions, which involve senior corporate management. While CEOs, especially in the larger corporations, may not get involved in details concerned with particular functional regulations, they must be concerned with the policies governing the responses of their company. One study of over 400 companies found a high and increasing incidence of top management involvement in decisions associated with government regulations.[5]

Third, as will be shown in the next and subsequent chapters, CEOs are becoming much more involved in the political processes through which regulations are promulgated, legislated, and administered.

Donald Rumsfeld, former Congressman (four terms), White House Chief of Staff for President Ford, Secretary of Defense, holder of other top-level government positions, and now CEO of G. D. Searle & Co., made some sobering comments about this issue:

> When I get up in the morning as a businessman, I think a lot more about government than I do about our competition, because government is that much involved—whether it's HEW, IRS, SEC, FTC, FDA. I always understood the problem intellectually, but the specific inefficiencies that result from the government's injecting itself into

practically every aspect of our business—this is something one can only feel by being here.[6]

James R. Shepley, the President of Time Inc., stated the reality of government's impact on business this way:

> The Battle of Washington is as important to the CEO as anything on his agenda—personnel, finance, litigation, production, marketing —you name it.[7]

One executive spelled out the changing role of the CEO of a large public utility in these words:

> For decades our main concerns were largely of a technical and engineering nature. As we started the 1970s, our industry was confronted with important changes: environmental concerns heightened; supplies of cheap and abundant natural gas and oil diminished; costs escalated dramatically; and the political response to these changes resulted in extensive legislation and a more pervasive regulatory process at both state and federal levels. The Chief Executive Officer became less a manager of the technical and engineering parts of our business and more a manager of the governmental, political, and public communications aspects.
>
> We were also beset in the early 1970s with very militant consumer activists, who lengthened rate-making proceedings, and single-interest environmental groups, who delayed—and even blocked—needed new energy projects. There were even local elections calling for a government takeover of major segments of our business.
>
> All these things required the CEO to spend much more time— perhaps a majority of his time—(a) meeting elected governmental officials, (b) carrying on a dialogue with regulatory officials, (c) participating in the legislative process, (d) communicating with the constituencies—business groups, shareholder groups, agricultural groups, and labor groups—that tend to identify their interests with ours, and (e) overseeing the drafting of the company's written communications with the public.[8]

The Community as a Priority for Attention

Business people from the very inception of this nation have been concerned with community affairs. A majority of the framers of our Constitution, for example, were from the business world. In a sweeping examination of the historical relationship of business and the community, Morrell Heald observed:

23

American businessmen fully shared the social concerns and preoccupations of their fellow citizens. Although they have often been depicted—indeed, caricatured—as single-minded pursuers of profit, the facts are quite otherwise. The nature of their activities often brought them into close contact with the harsher aspects of the life of a rapidly industrializing society. Like others, they were frequently troubled by the conditions they saw; and, also like others, they numbered in their ranks men who contributed both of their ideas and their resources to redress social imbalance and disorganization.[9]

Added to the natural concern of managers about community problems has been in recent years increasing pressure upon corporate managers by various constituents of the corporation to address community problems. Business people have responded so that today there is even greater participation of business in community affairs than ever before. This matter will be discussed further in later chapters. Here we wish only to make the point that this area has occupied more and more CEO time until today it is of substantial proportions for many of them.

What occupies the attention of the CEO outside the company varies. For example, on this point, William S. Sneath, when CEO of Union Carbide, said:

Fifteen years ago, the CEO of Union Carbide spent a good bit of time dealing with outside activities, including the federal government. I don't think you would find that the amount of time spent outside or inside has changed too much, but *what* is done outside has changed considerably. For example, more time is spent on public policy issues; Business Roundtable activities; giving talks on issues that are important to the academic community, business groups, and others; attending a governor's conference; and so on. Less time is being spent on traditional activities such as attending meetings of boards of directors of other companies. But in our company the change has been gradual over time, not abrupt.[10]

Today's CEO spends much more time outside of the office. As Donald Seibert, the CEO of J. C. Penney, stated:

I find myself out of the office more, and more involved in community affairs. I spend a great deal of time in Washington, either on behalf of the Business Roundtable, the Business Council, one of the trade associations that represent the retail industry, or particular interests of the Penney Company. I find more time being spent with industry groups, whether a trade association or an ad hoc group, in meetings to discuss strategy about what should be done, or to listen

24

to technical people explain particular situations. In addition, many of the things that were delegated to government relations people in the past have now become the direct concern of the CEO, and this too requires spending much time in briefings."[11]

Many CEOs today accept the fact, as noted by Mr. Seibert, that it is their responsibility to do things that in the past might have been delegated to a subordinate. One CEO commented:

> I can't tell you how many times I ask, "Well, do I have to be there?" and the answer is, "Yes." I am told: "Well, you don't have to be there, but it won't be as effective." So you go to give the testimony or make the speech. It isn't that the ability of the CEO is so much greater than that of other individuals who could go; it's the significance of the office. The presence of the CEO is seen as an indication that the company attaches a high level of importance to that particular matter.[12]

The fact that CEOs are spending much more of their time on matters outside their companies means, of course, that they are spending less on the traditional economic and technical affairs within. But involvement of time and skills in these external matters can produce the greatest payoff for the company. As Robert Cushman, the CEO of Norton Industries, put it:

> You are all aware that business management today is engaged in activities, problems and decisions that were virtually unheard of a generation ago. If you were to ask the heads of the nation's top 300 companies what factors would have the greatest influence on the future of their businesses in the coming decade, I suspect the vast majority would say *government and the force of public opinion on public policy*. All of our skills at managing—financial, manufacturing, marketing, research and development and the like—all these put together will not influence our destiny as much as what happens in political and economic arenas. As a consequence, managers of big institutions—whether they be presidents of corporations, universities, foundations or government agencies—must spend more time trying to understand and influence external affairs than they spend on the more traditional job of internal management.[13]

Pressures on the typical CEO to deal with external matters, together with the internal nuts and bolts of the business, require CEOs to spend most of their waking hours on business. They find few lulls in a day's work and a fast pace in the number of things that must be addressed.

Charles R. Dahl, the former CEO of Crown Zellerbach, said:

> There's only so much time. And each CEO has a different capacity for work. It doesn't make a difference whether that capacity is forty or eighty hours a week, if that's all one can work. The percentage that the CEO now spends in what I would think of as operating the business, the economic side of the business, has diminished tremendously, and more and more and more of his time is spent on the noneconomic aspects of the business. I'd have to say, however, that working on some of these noneconomic problems, in the long run, may mean more to the economics of the corporation than, say, running the day-to-day operations of a pulp mill.[14]

Concluding Observations

We have not sought to elaborate in this chapter all the different activities in the corporate environment that occupy the time of the typical CEO of our large companies. That will be done in later chapters. Here, our point is that half the typical CEO's time is generally devoted to dealing with environmental forces of which the government and the community are dominant concerns. This is a much higher percentage, and a different emphasis, than even a few years ago.

3

A Strategy of
CEO Involvement
in External Affairs

Underlying the increasing expenditure of time by the typical CEO on matters that affect the company from outside have been two significant modifications of what are perceived to be CEO responsibilities. One is that the interests of the corporation will be better protected by the active involvement of the CEO in external sociopolitical processes. The other is a new and deepening concern for the legitimate interests of major constituencies of the enterprise. The first is the subject of this chapter. The second will be dealt with in the next chapter.

Traditionally, the strategy of the majority of top business executives in the United States has been one of maintaining a low profile in the public forum and an intractable position against governmental initiatives. Even casual consideration of the mountain of government regulation of business and of the low level of credibility that business enjoys today attests convincingly to the disastrous consequences of that strategy. To be sure, the bite of government regulations today and the low regard in which big business is generally held in this society are not alone due to the reluctance of business people to become involved in public policy processes nor to their frequent stubborn resistance to new proposed regulations, but it has been an important influence in shaping the public's low level of respect for business and the government's high level of control.[1]

Today, the strategy employed by the CEOs in many corporations, including those sampled in this survey, is just the reverse. It is one of active involvement in the public policy processes and new initiatives to communicate with the constituents of business. This strategy has profoundly altered the managerial job of the CEO and the internal decision-making processes and organization of the large corporation.

By this observation we do not mean to imply that business leaders did not speak out in the past nor seek to communicate with constituent interests. Indeed, they did occasionally, but there was no general, conscious, and purposeful strategy to do so as there is today. Also, as we shall see, the perception of "constituent interests" has changed significantly in recent years.

The forces initiating and supporting a strategy of CEO involvement have been many and complex. The more important ones are described below in the words of CEOs. The various motivating forces that are given below are not mutually exclusive nor are they all of the same level of importance. Many of them interrelate with, and reinforce, one another. It is important to observe, too, that while some of them seem defensive and self-serving, there are others that are primarily public spirited.

Increased Attention to Public Policy

The changing business environment demands high and proactive attention. As Reginald H. Jones, then the CEO of General Electric, put it:

> The most intractable problems facing business today are those that are external to the company. Public policy determines whether our enterprise system can survive and whether individual companies will have a climate in which they can prosper and make their full contribution. The CEO, as designated leader of the corporation, has to participate actively in the formation of public policy affecting business. And I do that, even though it takes something like half of my available time—either in preparation or in actual spokesmanship and personal representation in Washington. The time has been well spent, I think, not only in waking up the country to economic problems that had

been long neglected, but also in terms of positive customer, investor, and employee relations. These duties are part and parcel of the CEO's responsibilities for the strategic direction of the company.[2]

While external issues get top billing, said the late Louis B. Lundborg, the former CEO of the Bank of America,

> ... even the most internal concerns, when examined, prove to be largely a response and reaction to changes in the environment and climate in which today's corporation is operating.[3]

CEOs of the larger corporations today accept a responsibility to be a positive force in the social and political arena. This is not solely a matter of defending the corporation but involves a deep interest in resolving major social problems, injecting more economic rationality into the political processes, helping to assure that our sociopolitical system works better in the interests of everyone, and preserving political and economic freedom. A number of CEOs have commented on this point.

Robert S. Hatfield, then the CEO of the Continental Group, declared that management must become a part of the political process:

> ... beyond concern for quality of operations, worklife, and character, it is now also apparent to a growing number of chief executive officers that they and their associates in management must, as a part of their jobs, be a positive force in the political process of this country. They realize that effective internal operations will come to naught if pervasive government destroys, by regulation and control, the ability to compete in the marketplace and maintain the financial strength of the business. Boards of directors, in their increasing responsibility to the shareholders, are beginning to become more sensitive to the performance of top management in the political process. More and more corporate citizenship is being considered an important part of management's responsibility.[4]

Irving S. Shapiro has written that the corporation has obligations beyond satisfying stockholder interests, a matter that will be considered in more detail in the next section.

> I think we're a means to an end, and while producing goods and providing jobs is our primary function, we can't live successfully in a society if the hearts of its cities are decaying and its people can't support their families. We've got to help make the whole system work,

and that involves more than just having a safe workplace and providing jobs for the number of people we hire. It means that just as you
want libraries, and you want schools, and you want fire departments
and police departments, you also want businesses to help do something about unsolved social problems.[5]

Thomas A. Murphy, when he was the CEO of General Motors,
underscored this position in these words:

Business still has to satisfy customers because if you don't have
customers, you don't have a business. In satisfying customers you've
got to have the products, you've got to compete in the marketplace,
and you've got to make a little money in the process because that's
what the stockholders expect you to do. At the same time, you have
to relate to the problems of the communities in which you live; you
have to do the things that you're expected to do; you have to be a good
citizen.[6]

A Concern for a Balance of Power

*While not frequently articulated, a powerful motive for increased
attention to public policy is to counterbalance the power of government.* Business is one of the most potentially powerful checks
on the unrestrained increase and exercise of governmental pow-
ers, and if it neglects to become a voice in public debate it will, as
it has discovered, forfeit influencing decision-making so that politicians will be influenced by special interests other than business.
A good bit of current legislation that restricts business is a result
of a lack of consensus among business leaders, reluctance of business people to become involved in public policy debate, and the
absence of constructive choices in public issues that could be presented by business.

The counterweight of business in the political arena, observed
Robert Hatfield, is needed, not only to have the business voice
heard but also to help preserve individual political and economic
freedoms.

I find myself devoting as much as half of my time in various aspects
of what we've come to call "corporate citizenship," which includes
not only political involvement but also involvement with social matters generally. In the government area, I try to contribute to better

legislation and sounder policy; in other societal areas, I try to impress on everybody that the ultimate issue is freedom of the individual.[7]

This is a point that has been emphasized by Richard Eells, Professor of Business in the Graduate School of Business at Columbia University:

> Ultimately, the question of government control over private enterprise is intimately tied to the fate of the rights of the individual and the political freedoms on which our political system is based. A historic tradition now extending back some 500 years—and even further, in embryonic form—has welded freedom from arbitrary acts of government with the right of private economic activity. Without a system of private associations to counterbalance the powers of public government, the society is threatened by the same bureaucratic and authoritarian strangulation that we see in many places around the world.[8]

The Need to Improve Public Confidence in Business

CEOs believe that there is a great need to reduce biased criticism of business, reverse current low levels of confidence in business, and erase misunderstandings of the ways a large corporation operates. They see a need to educate people about what business really is and to clarify the concept of what it should be. Executives see a challenge to the very legitimacy of the corporation. As Louis B. Lundborg wrote:

> Along with the other difficulties that are making their job of management difficult, executives are disturbed by what they see as a challenge to the legitimacy of their corporations. Legitimacy—the public perception that business is serving a societal need—is the charter under which business must operate in a democratic society. Without it, corporations will be strangled by legislation, regulation, or in the extreme, nationalization. Business legitimacy is being questioned on two broad fronts—its conduct, structure, and attitude as an institution, and its performance as a supplier of goods and services to the public. In both areas, the atmosphere can be described as one of substantial, and in many quarters growing, mistrust.[9]

Strengthening legitimacy involves not only better economic and technical performance but, in the views of many CEOs, better communications with people generally. James Affleck, the CEO of American Cyanamid, observed that:

> I think the thing that will help the most will be giving the public a better understanding of the corporation and profit, and how jobs are created. We need to put a lot of work into economic education.[10]

Edmund W. Littlefield, the CEO of Utah International, added this:

> In devising strategies to cope with the new conditions of the 80's, chief executives in the United States start with the premise that it is necessary to create a new level of business acceptance and legitimacy that is attuned to the socio-political demands of the 80's. Managements are moving from a posture of simply reacting to external forces to a mode of anticipating the issues and even helping to shape the issues.[11]

Thomas Murphy has said that business has not done well in promoting its ideas.

> We business people are usually at our best when we are making something, or selling something, or servicing something—and competing with other companies at every step along the way. We thrive on competition. We know more about it than anyone else. We're experts. We live and breathe competition every day. That's when we're competing in the conventional marketplace of goods and services. But there is another marketplace out there—the marketplace of ideas and of public issues. This is a marketplace which we haven't penetrated nearly so well—not as we should have and not as we *could* have. The truth is that we have been clobbered. As a result, we have not been able to do our best in the more traditional areas of competition as well. Our freedom of action has been restricted.[12]

Reginald Jones has added a supporting opinion: "We're convinced that the corporation as we know it will not continue to exist unless we do a better job of defining and explaining its role in society."[13] He developed this point in a statement he made at an Indiana Graduate School of Business conference:

> Regaining and sustaining legitimacy is not a simple matter. It involves a wide range of actions by business. Included is better performance with respect to products and service, more sensitivity to the social goals of society, visibility on the public scene, an improved theory and practice of corporate governance, the development of a

business constituency who will defend the corporation in times of trouble and speak up for it in the debates over public policy, and the personal participation of executives in the formation of public policy.[14]

The Need for Business-Government Cooperation

CEOs believe that the traditional adversary relationship between business and government, which frequently has been encrusted with deep antipathy on both sides, should be abandoned in favor of more cooperation and understanding. They express different reasons for this posture and suggest different relationships that it might involve. For example, Irving Shapiro has noted the unproductive past relationship and the more promising cooperative relationship in these words:

> Those of us in business management and those who will come into these jobs in the future have an obligation to help the public policy process where possible—recognizing our own limitations, but realizing too that we can go a long way toward improving the climate between business and government and ending the ancient, mutually destructive, and non-productive animosity that has too long discolored the American political and economic environment.[15]

Most CEOs in this sample agree with Ruben F. Mettler, the CEO of TRW, that appropriate business-government cooperation is essential if we are to develop wise public policy:

> Unfortunately, past experience suggests that a national cohesive [economic] policy is not likely to be conceived by the government alone in a timely fashion. A new source of initiative and sustained effort is required to make it happen. That impetus can best—and probably only—come from the private sector.
> Private business—large and small—can and, in my opinion, should provide more support for a continuing effort of research, study, persuasion, advocacy and plain hard lobbying for cohesive, long-range economic policies. The resources of individual companies and of the important research and advocacy groups can be used to develop positive proposals and promote their adoption. Where management and technological expertise are central to the development of public policy, business and other private institutions can lend their experience to political leaders to help them understand how the market system works most effectively, and—equally important—what won't work.[16]

On the other hand, Irving Shapiro has said that business must understand governmental processes and learn to live with them:

> . . . business executives are learning to live with their common law partner. They are taking a few bruises in the bargain, but that is a small price to pay for an on-the-job education in how the public policy process works and how to figure out what is practical and what is not. The central fact is that executives now see this as something they have to learn to run their businesses properly and to make the American system work better—as much a duty for a business executive as for anyone else.[17]

It is to the advantage of government to get information from business, and it is in the interest of business to be as constructive as possible, Richard Landis, the CEO of Del Monte, asserted:

> Agencies of government often look to business for advice and counsel. There is an understanding in many of the government agencies that unexpected complications can arise from regulations. The potential impact of regulations demands careful consideration. We can help this consideration by providing government agencies the facts of our experiences, thereby enabling them to make informed decisions.
>
> Also, we can suggest possible alternative solutions. If we sit back and wait until an agency says, "Well, here's what you're going to do," we may end up with the worst possible situation. A much better approach is to step forward and say, "Here's a viable and constructive program that addresses the problem and solves it in a practical manner." A program that serves the needs of the consumer and renders suitable regulation is much more likely to evolve when business provides its constructive input to the regulatory process.[18]

The past Chairman of Union Carbide, William S. Sneath, points out that there are limits to what the free market mechanism can do and instances where business should invite government help. In a speech before the Town Hall of California in 1980, he said:

> At Union Carbide, we have been encouraging government to provide economic incentives that would make it possible to expand investment in industrial energy conservation projects. Now this might be heretical to economic purists who bridle at every new invitation to government to intervene in the marketplace. But conservation energy is the lowest-cost new energy the nation can buy, and without government incentives, industry cannot soon conserve at the level that would otherwise be possible.
>
> So . . . it makes a good deal more sense—for us and for the nation

—to invite government help than to stand on our free-market principles.[19]

CEOs do recognize that government not only has the right to
regulate business but has plenty of reason for doing so. The issue
is not regulation per se but what CEOs consider to be unwise,
unjust, irresponsible, conflicting, and uneconomic regulation. A.
W. Clausen, the former CEO of the Bank of America, addressed
this point:

> Few in our society would question the government's right—indeed,
> its duty—to regulate business. The market mechanism has its flaws
> and distortions, and our democratic society has needs that are not
> always fulfilled by the incentives that capitalism normally provides.
> What we must question in this time of economic stagnation and
> malfunction is the amount, the efficiency, and the logic of present-
> day regulation.[20]

Franklin Murphy, the CEO of the Times Mirror Company, added:

> There has to be a strong governmental presence today. My problem
> is not with regulation per se; it is with overregulation, blind regula-
> tion, stupid regulation. We have a regulatory system that isn't ac-
> countable to anybody.[21]

"The aim [of business]," William Sneath has remarked, "should
not be to stop regulation in its tracks, but only to make it more
efficient, less costly, and better attuned to the nation's needs. Both
social and economic values will be better served.[22]

The CEO of Rockwell International, Robert Anderson, said: "The
time has come to renew and extend the partnership between government and business that has led to so many great achievements
in the past."[23]

But none of these CEOs have in mind anything approaching a
mutual back-scratching operation. Said Irving Shapiro:

> It is healthy to keep business and government at arm's length, with
> each behaving in such a way that neither would mind the facts being
> reported in the newspapers. However, an arm's length relationship
> doesn't require the kind of hostility we have seen in recent years.[24]

Fletcher L. Byrom, the CEO of Koppers Company, reiterates this
position:

We must take the meaning of "the enemy" out of the traditional concept of the adversary relationship of business and government. But this does not mean full and complete cooperation and accommodation. There should be *some* tension in the relationship. We need more ad hoc groups to work with government in dealing with our problems. Such groups have the virtue of being self-destructive; after finishing their job, they go out of business.[25]

The Inevitability of Involvement

Finally, there is the belief that there is no alternative but deep involvement in the sociopolitical process. Survival depends on intelligent participation in that process. This is implicit in much that has been said above and much that will be discussed later. John Hoving, Senior Vice President of Federated Department Stores, summarized the need for business in a pluralistic society to get involved, saying that:

Since this is a democracy becoming more participatory all the time, there is no hope at all that governments will leave corporations alone. A distinguished political scientist, Harold Lasswell, used to teach that politics is the story of who gets what, when, where, and how. This society of ours is a pluralism in which powerful forces are constantly battling for the control and allocation of productive resources. That's what the political process is all about, and if you do not take part with all your wit and imagination, you will be told by someone else or some institution just what to do. There is no way in which a corporation can say to this political world: "Stop! I want to get off!"[26]

Concluding Observations

In Chapter 2 it was observed that today's CEOs spend a very large and increasing amount of their time dealing with external environmental forces. One major reason for this shift in emphasis is the new strategy of CEOs of our large corporations to get involved in the public policy processes, and this chapter noted the many reasons why CEOs believe they should be directly involved in public policy making. Another important reason for increasing attention to external affairs is the decision by the typical CEO to respond to all legitimate constituent interests. This strategy is examined in the next chapter.

4

The Strategy of Positive Response to Legitimate Constituent Interests

MANY CEOs of large companies in the past believed that they were trustees for major constituent interests and that their companies had a responsibility that went beyond the strictly economic one of seeking to optimize the short-term returns of the common stockholder. Thus, the current strategy of responding positively to the legitimate interests of the various constituents of the corporation is by no means a new invention. However, the full meaning of this strategy today is far different from the meaning it had as recently as twenty years ago.

CEO Views of Constituent Interests

For example, David Rockefeller, the recently retired CEO of Chase Manhattan Bank, in his McKinsey Foundation Lecture in 1964 at Columbia University said:

> The old concept that the owner of a business had a right to use his property as he pleased to maximize profits has evolved into the belief that ownership carries certain binding social obligations. Today's

manager serves as trustee not only for the owners but for the workers and indeed for our entire society. As a nation of wage and salaried people, we work in the main for business organizations. Business recruits our youth from college and provides them with pensions in their old age. It contributes major support to charitable institutions, and has become a principal source of funds for the growth and improvement of our colleges and universities. Corporations have developed a sensitive awareness of their responsibility for maintaining an equitable balance among the claims of stockholders, employees, customers, and the public at large.[1]

This belief was shared by other McKinsey lecturers such as Ralph Cordiner, then president of General Electric, Thomas Watson, Jr.,[2] then CEO of IBM, and by many business leaders of our larger corporations. This was by no means a new belief in 1964 when David Rockefeller enunciated it.

The interpretation given to that statement then, however, was considerably narrower than today. David Rockefeller recently said that today's corporation is expected by society to help to improve the quality of life, a concept that certainly was in the minds of CEOs twenty years ago but not nearly as strongly or in as great detail as it is today. Similarly, CEOs of the past favored equal opportunity, the advancement of women in organizations, and a recognition of broad community responsibilities, but nowhere near as strongly as today.[3]

We asked Charles R. Dahl, the then President and CEO of Crown Zellerbach, about David Rockefeller's statement that corporations have developed a "sensitive awareness" of their responsibilities for balancing constituent interests. He responded:

> I think that nearly all responsible and perceptive corporations have long been sensitive to constituent interests and the need to address them in ways that are fair and responsive.
>
> What has happened in recent years is simply that the issues have sharpened and multiplied. Various constituent groups have organized, have become vocal, and are more aggressive in seeking responses that match their own objectives. As a result, the issues and demands receive much more publicity and public attention now. We are certainly sensitive today to issues that were not of general concern in the past.
>
> Saying it differently, corporations do try to be aware of social trends and embryonic issues. But until there is sufficient evolution of the thought process among the various constituencies to clearly define the issues, the corporation is not in a position to make an appropriate response.

It is also true that we can't be sensitive to all the dormant issues that might in time emerge as quite important. The test of responsibility is whether we are actually making an effort to identify such matters and to determine whether we have a present, constructive role to play in the formative process. At the same time we must deal squarely and fairly with issues that have in fact emerged as important and which deserve a corporate response.[4]

As John D. deButts pointed out, when he was the CEO of American Telephone and Telegraph, the interests with which CEOs of large corporations today must cope are many and raise problems for appropriate corporate response:

I can recall the time when it was common to use the analogy of a three-legged stool to make the point that management's role was, in fact, to seek and maintain a balance of interests among just three constituencies—customers, shareowners, and employees. I am told that in the 1950s, Thomas J. Watson, Sr., then chairman of the board of IBM, insisted upon systematically changing the order in which he mentioned those three constituencies in successive talks and speeches. That was his method of stressing their equality.

But times have changed and we seldom hear of three-legged stools anymore.

I have tried, unsuccessfully, to think of what would serve as a modern day replacement for our now outdated three-legged stool. The only image which recurs with uncomfortable persistence is not a piece of furniture at all. It's a porcupine—with the quills reversed.

For to the traditional constituencies of business have since been added a whole host of new constituencies encompassing the interest, general and specific, of the entire public and those who speak or profess to speak in its behalf; legislators, regulators, consumer advocates, environmentalists, activists of just about every kind and persuasion. In attempting to balance the diverse demands of such varied constituencies, all that today's managers can be certain of is that what best serves everybody will meet the perfect satisfaction of nobody. Nonetheless they try.[5]

The concept of the manager as trustee has evolved into a strategy of identifying major external interests from all sources that affect a corporation today, and may possibly in the future, and framing an appropriate response to those, which, in the judgment of top management, should be addressed.

Without exception the CEOs interviewed for this study accept a responsibility for responding as best they can to the social, as distinct from the economic and technical, forces exerted by individuals and groups on the corporation. Let us cite five of these CEOs who have previously published their views on this business responsibility. The scope of their concern is expressed in different ways but carries a common thread. Thornton Bradshaw, then the President of ARCO and now the CEO of RCA, was quoted by the Los Angeles *Herald Examiner* in 1979 as saying:

> We have a basic philosophy that a corporation has two roles to play, and it cannot survive without playing both those roles. The first role is the economic role, providing quality goods and services that the public wants at the lowest possible price and making an acceptable rate of return on its investment. Beyond that, the corporation today is more than just an economic unit, it is also part of our society. And, therefore, more is expected from it than just making a profit.[6]

Randall Meyer, the President of Exxon Company, U.S.A., in an address given at the University of Chicago in 1977, stated that:

> Business must evidence, for example, in its every action that it is willing and able to respond to the ever-growing concern of the American people for the interests, needs and rights of individuals in society. This is true whether that concern is expressed in terms of the individual's right to clean air, to safe working conditions, to equal employment opportunities, or to his or her right as a citizen to have a government free of the undue interference of special interests.
>
> Business must extend its involvement as well into community needs and interests. Companies are expected to recognize their obligations to support educational and cultural institutions. And, again, there are logical business reasons for a company to respond to the best of its ability to these expectations. . . . In sum, business managers have the responsibility to understand what society expects of their enterprise, and to insure that the enterprise measures up.[7]

In a speech to a United Fund dinner in 1979, William M. Ellinghouse, the President and Chief Operating Officer of American Telephone and Telegraph, said:

> Business is now held accountable for its actions by a host of vocal, well-organized constituents: regulators, community leaders, competitors, environmentalists, consumerists, minorities and countless others. Business' response, it seems to me, is that we can claim no right except what we earn through performance. And only by matching our performance to society's expectations can we confirm the legitimacy of corporate goals and motivations.[8]

A. W. Clausen, when the CEO of the Bank of America, wrote:

> The health of our communities is recognized as directly related to business success. Executives don't relegate it to separate, occasional study sessions. We live and work with the questions of environment, minorities, affordable health care, vocational opportunities, community safety day in and day out, because they are part and parcel of making intelligent and effective business decisions.[9]

Finally, Irving S. Shapiro, the former Chairman and CEO of du Pont, said in a lecture at Carnegie-Mellon University in 1979:

> It is no longer considered enough for a company to make products and provide commercial services. The larger it is, the more it is expected to assume various obligations that once were met by individuals or communities, or were not met at all.[10]

The CEO's Dual Responsibility

There is no question at all about the fact that the CEOs of the largest corporations have formulated a strategy of responsiveness to the noneconomic as well as the economic forces that they confront in their work. By their words and their actions, which we will discuss later in this report, they show that they recognize that noneconomic forces are as potent in fashioning corporate behavior as are economic forces. They believe that they must respond as best they can to legitimate public demands. They accept the view that the worst possible strategy would be one that is perceived by the public generally as being nonresponsive, if not in opposition, to important interests of society. Since a society has the ultimate power to shape the conditions under which business functions, it would hardly be a good strategy to permit a company to be so perceived. Today's CEOs believe that a strong and viable business system will not exist in a society where a majority of the public perceive the interests of the business corporation as being opposed to the social interests of the public. While there is no consensus about what all of the social responsibilities of business are, there is no doubt that the CEOs of the largest corporations see the very survival of the business institution particularly resting on a response that is accepted by the more moderate members of society.

This is what John deButts had in mind when he wrote:

41

And no longer are society's wants and needs vis-a-vis business measured strictly in terms of marketplace demand. Instead, the corporation is now viewed as having a wide variety of responsibilities transcending the marketplace. Some of these responsibilities are in society at large. Whether a business has social responsibilities is, I know, a subject of widespread debate. But to my mind, it is a debate that continues long after the argument is over. Today I know of no leader of business who sees his function as limited to the pursuit of profit. I know of none who does not realize that the business that for profit's sake ignores the impacts of its actions on society is not likely to make a profit very long.[11]

Top managers of our corporations believe, and rightly so, that the corporation is and should be fundamentally an economic institution. The drive for increased profits is a dominant motivating objective. Profit consciousness, however, does not in and of itself exclude social consciousness. The two, rather, are closely related. As A. W. Clausen put it:

Individuals of widely differing backgrounds and interests, both inside and outside the business community, now openly acknowledge that profits and social goals are merely two sides of the same coin. This growing acceptance of the premise that we can't have social gains without economic gains, and vice versa, is of far-reaching importance. Properly tended and encouraged, it holds out the prospect of a broad consensus of national purpose that has been lacking, or at least obscured, in our debates about business and society over the past generation.[12]

The CEO of General Foods Corporation, James L. Ferguson, observed that his concern is focused on the long-term growth and profitability of his company. He then continues:

The primary role of the chief executive regarding the social obligations of his company or any other obligations is to make sure that he understands, and his organization understands, the basic nature of the business and how it relates to the needs and concerns of society. That is the core around which all other relationships are shaped. Without that core, I frankly don't know how other priorities can be set or other accomplishments measured.

If the first job of the chief executive is to see that the corporate identity and direction are established and understood, the second is to take the lead in defining the obligations that emanate from that and to spark the action necessary to meet those obligations.

From a conceptual standpoint, the other obligations are as easy to list as the Ten Commandments:

> Thou shalt not pollute the environment, and where
>   possible should beautify it.
> Thou shalt not injure employees, and if possible will see
>   that they are healthier.
> Thou shalt not sell products that are hazardous, and will
>   make every effort to see that they are beneficial.
> Thou shalt not deny opportunity to anybody, and will try to
>   create opportunity for everybody.
> Thou shalt be a good citizen, contribute to worthwhile
>   causes, and otherwise play a constructive role in the
>   communities and in the society in which you operate.

Those are the basic principles. The problem is how to apply them.[13]

In a speech in 1975, Thomas A. Murphy, the then CEO of General Motors, commented on the balancing of corporate economic interests with society's noneconomic demands:

> The real questions about corporate responsibility are: responsible for what? . . . and to whom? . . . and, most critically, who is to decide? The answers are by no means clear—not in my mind at least. Nor do I find much consensus in the authorities I read. The spectrum of opinion is broad. On one end is the strict fundamentalist doctrine of profit maximization. This holds management deficient if it engages in any activity that does not contribute directly to the profitability of the corporation. On the other side are those who say that the corporation's activity as a part—and a vital part—of the community should take precedence over its ability to turn a profit. These are extremes, and simplifications perhaps, but both views are strongly held.
> In practice, of course, the businessman knows that the road of right decision requires a proper reconcilement of these extremes. The long-term interest of a business requires conformity with society's changing demands—even those expressed outside the marketplace—just as the necessity to prosper in order to stay in business rules out total altruism. . . .
> To those who carry the responsibilities of management, to those who every day seek the balance among the obligations we owe to our stockholders, our employees, our customers, and to society as a whole, to those I point out that there need not be a conflict between seeking a profit and meeting the social and environmental demands of our people. It may even be, I suggest, that upon our ability to respond to these demands depends the preservation of free enterprise itself.[14]

The late Neil H. Jacoby, a professor of business at UCLA, held that: "The popular notion [in many academic economic circles] that a company which pursues profit must eschew a social role, or that social involvement means a sacrifice of profit, is unfounded.

On the contrary," he wrote, "the contemporary corporation must become socially involved in order to maximize its profit." [15]

In commenting on this same matter, Irving Shapiro has said that "corporations have a duty to help make a better society as well as a better product, and that this is not a bad way to maximize profits long range." [16]

In connection with the relationship between the economic and social performance of a corporation, a recent policy statement of the Business Roundtable made two points worthy of repetition here:

> . . . economic responsibility is by no means incompatible with other corporate responsibilities in society. In contemporary society all corporate responsibilities are so interrelated that they should not and cannot be separated. [17]
>
> A corporation's responsibilities include how the whole business is conducted every day. It must be a thoughtful institution which rises above the bottom line to consider the impact of its actions on all, from shareholders to the society at large. Its business activities must make social sense just as its social activities must make business sense. [18]

The executives in the sample on which this study is based were asked whether they found any important conflicts between their economic drives and the assumption of social responsibilities. Their response was negative. They had little trouble, they said, in reconciling the two. Perhaps they could deny a conflict because, as successful managers, they were able to put firm limits on the extent to which they engaged voluntarily in social programs so that there would not be a negative effect on their companies' economic performance.

Balancing Corporate Obligations

James Ferguson said, in commenting on balancing the different obligations of a corporation, that:

> The key lies in recognizing that there is a definite mix of motives in this area. On the one hand, there is clearly an "enlightened corporate self-interest" in being a fair employer, a reliable supplier, a law-abiding citizen, and a good neighbor. Regardless of how enlightened that self-interest may be, however, it is still self-interest. It is neither healthy nor wise to claim otherwise. We should not attempt to fool

44

ourselves or the public on this point, nor should we adopt an attitude of moral superiority. If a company fails to act as a good citizen and a good neighbor, sooner or later there will be a reaction which will affect its ability to function effectively. No responsible manager can afford to overlook that fact.

At the same time most of us do feel, and certainly should feel, a genuine human obligation, independent of any business motive, to help those who are in need and to contribute where we can to a better world. Within reasonable limits, I see no conflict between those motives. The key word, however, is *limits*.[19]

Irving Shapiro has warned about corporations going overboard in pursuing noneconomic programs:

> . . . there should be concern about corporations overreaching. It is not necessarily callous or antisocial to raise doubts about the competence of business managers to accept all the tasks pushed at them, and to ask what legitimizes their appointment to social office.
>
> Sometimes business seems to be drafted because it is presumed to have a deep pocket, and because society is looking for a place to dump problems. Because they have done well at economic missions, corporations may be presumed by some to be equally qualified for many other tasks, but that is a risky assumption.
>
> The point here is not to argue one position or another in the social responsibility debate, but only to suggest that with public expectations ratcheting upward, corporations are under pressure to behave more like governments and embrace a universe of problems. That would mean, of necessity, that private institutions would focus less on problems of their own choice. If corporations succumbed to that pressure, and in effect declared the public's work to be their own, the next step would be to turn them into institutions accountable to the public in the same way that units of government are accountable. Suppose that happened. What difference would it make? Apart from the philosophical difficulties (can you have a free society if its economic engine is predominantly under government direction?), there are practical questions of efficiency.[20]

Concluding Observations

It should be repeated that this report expresses the views of the CEOs sampled for this survey. There are many CEOs, even of some large corporations, who believe that they are discharging their social responsibilities completely when they manage their companies efficiently in producing products and services that the public will buy. And the CEOs of this sample accept the idea that a company is being socially responsible when it operates efficiently —but they go beyond that. They believe that as corporations grow larger, the social programs that they undertake voluntarily become more and more necessary and important. Indeed, as many of them were quoted as saying, their companies will not be able to optimize long-range stockholder returns unless they do take on such social programs.

They realize that there is, however, a limit to what they can and should be doing in the social area. They also recognize that today —and in the foreseeable future—the great bulk of the social programs that they do undertake are—and will be—mandated by the government. So, while they talk about responding positively and voluntarily to legitimate constituent interests, they are addressing only a small part of their total social responsibilities. Nevertheless, the philosophical difference between their accepting voluntarily constituent pressures to pursue social programs and their denying that they have any obligations to do so is very great and important.

5

New Managerial Qualities
Required of the CEO

As the world of business has evolved in recent decades it has become clear that a new range of managerial talent had come to be necessary for success. To get some first-hand insight into the changes that had taken place we asked many of the CEOs in our interview sample what qualities were required in CEOs of large corporations to meet the challenges facing their organizations today. In particular, we said we wanted to know what qualities were needed to assure the most effective operations of their companies and the survival of the free enterprise business institution. In what follows we have tried to draw a composite of their responses. In addition, we have included the thinking of some CEOs on this subject as expressed in their speeches and written materials, along with some of our own observations.

It will readily be seen that a few of the qualities are not new. In some cases, new dimensions are added to old qualities. But some of the qualities mentioned are new. Altogether, however, they define a new class of CEO. The qualities that were mentioned were not discrete. Many of them are linked, and many can be classified as subspecies of others. In our discussion of these qualities we will give somewhat more attention to the newer characteristics. Hence, the space devoted to a particular quality does not signify the degree of importance relative to other managerial requirements that we assign to it. Nor is the order in which the qualities are listed of particular significance.

Administrative Ability

First, the CEO must have a thorough knowledge of the economic and technical characteristics of his or her business. This is, of course, a traditional quality required of CEOs. All CEOs commenting on this characteristic underscored its importance. They had in mind not only the external economic and technical influences on their companies but also the internal operational characteristics of their businesses. While their attention is being focused more and more on the major external environmental forces affecting their companies, they believe it is very important for them to have a firm grasp of the internal economic and technical aspects of their companies. They believe this knowledge is essential if their decision making and leadership is to be creditable, both inside and outside their organizations.

Second, the CEO must be an astute administrator. Skillful administration, of course, has many dimensions. An effective CEO has always needed this ability, but because of the new forces focused on the business corporation today, the demands of administration have altered. Certainly, the managerial task has become much more complicated today than ever before. CEOs must grapple with the many different new constituent interests that have gained a voice in recent years. Managers today are required to make many important decisions in a shorter period of time than in the past. While more information is available in many areas than before, there is often not much time to collect and analyze it. Astute administration today involves an ability to integrate traditional decision-making criteria (principally economic and technical) with new qualitative criteria stemming from the surrounding society (for example, social responsibilities). Beyond these dimensions are others such as those pointed out by A. W. Clausen in these words:

> There are some things about good managers that we take for granted. A good manager has intelligence, drive, determination, staying power, and a great desire to do the right thing—and do it well in ways that are sensitive to the needs, capacities and expectations of others.[1] In

sum, the CEO must be able to "run the store" efficiently and effectively.

Leadership

Third, the CEO must be a leader. CEO leadership means the capability of influencing people in the organization to willingly and enthusiastically follow in achieving the objectives of the enterprise. In today's world this often means leading them to becoming more sensitive to the social and political factors affecting them and the enterprise, and in participating in community and political processes. Most of the CEOs in the sample for this study accepted the view that CEOs must not only be able to inspire their own employees but also be influential on the public platform. In short, the CEO must have a certain amount of charisma.

The quality of leadership has to be distinguished from that of astute administration, although they are closely related. As Fletcher Byrom put it:

> The CEO must be a leader rather than an administrator of the status quo. He must be a leader in the sense of being an "enabler," that is, one who helps others to get their job done well. The CEO must be capable of envisioning the future and leading the corporation toward it most efficiently. He must have the charisma that will inspire others to enthusiastic support and effort.[2]

Sensitivity to Social and Political Forces

Fourth, the CEO must be sensitive to the social and political forces that affect the company. The strategy of concern about forces external to the corporation was discussed previously, but a few more comments on the subject relevant to the work of the CEO deserve attention.

Franklin Murphy observed in our interview:

> Ten years ago my primary preoccupation was with growth and profit, primarily over a relatively short term. Today, my obligation is to remind my colleagues that there are forces other than the drive for profits that we must consider. Let's not start down some acquisition road without considering fully all of its implications—not just the project projections—for many years in the future.[3]

A. W. Clausen set forth the need to be sensitive and responsive in these words:

> Those of us responsible for the management of large corporations operate on a mandate from our several constituencies: most directly, our customers—but also our shareholders, employees, our legislators and regulators and the general public. Which is why I'm so strongly convinced that part of our job is to remain responsive to their needs and wishes and to preserve their understanding and good will.[4]

At the Bank of America, a major criterion for promotion of managers is sensitivity to the environment in which the bank operates. At General Electric, Reginald Jones has said, lack of sensitivity to environmental forces will block advancement. He noted:

> Our political-social-economic environment is changing. Business has to prepare to meet these new situations. When it comes to top executive prospects, I have had my disappointments. I have had some individuals who I thought had extraordinarily high IQ's, great capabilities, great industry and diligence, high ethics and morality—but they were lacking in sensitivity. We just had to say, "Well that individual is not going to deal effectively with some of the problems he will be facing. We will just have to drop him from consideration."[5]

CEOs recognize that there are threats as well as opportunities in the changing sociopolitical environment. Richard C. Gerstenberg, when Chairman of General Motors Corporation, put it this way:

> The most successful business in the years ahead will be the one that not only offers quality products at competitive prices, but also succeeds in matching its resources to society's changing demands, the business that is best able to give creative response to the social aspirations of the people it serves. Conversely, the business that fails in the years ahead will be the one that fails to understand how it is related to the society around it and will therefore overlook opportunities for service, for growth, and for profit.[6]

Ability to Balance Constituent Interests

Fifth, the CEO must have the ability to balance appropriately the legitimate interests of major constituents of the business. It is one thing to be sensitive to environmental forces. It is quite another to balance, in the decision-making process, the traditional economic and technical considerations with the noneconomic interests of the external as well as internal constituents of the company. The skill of balancing such interests is daily becoming more and more important for the typical CEO and is dramatically changing his managerial task. This new aspect of the management job was discussed earlier, but in this context we can usefully make a few additional points about it.

The demand to balance all constituent interests is a genuine innovation in the managerial task. It is complicated by the need for making many different cost/benefit analyses, weighing many different constituent demands and company obligations, and making a variety of trade-offs in the final decisions. Louis Lundborg described the new requirement in these words:

> The effective executive in the years just ahead will be one who does not neglect his company's operating efficiency and its profit-making goals but who from the outset puts those targets into their proper perspective. In a degree that few of his predecessors have done, he will see his company and his industry as part of a society that has a stake in everything his company does. He will recognize that he (his company) has responsibilities to that society, and to each of the other stakeholders identified above. He will still be concerned with his "bottom line," but he will not be able to treat it in a vacuum. He will have the very difficult, and at times painful, task of resolving conflicts and making trade-offs between the opposing expectations of those stakeholders before he arrives at his bottom line; how much to employees and how much to owners; how much to customers in lower prices or higher quality; for employees, how much now in wages and salaries, and how much for pensions and other "fringes"; for the owners, how much in dividends and how much plowed back into future earning power; and above all, how much to all of these, and how much to be spent along the way in meeting his obligations to society: first in internal, mainstream operations to make sure that he is living up to society's standards as to pollution and other environmental elements, as to employment practices, and as to ethical conduct; and then to make sure that the company is doing its fair share to meet the problem of the community or communities in which it operates.[7]

The stake in doing a good job, in Lundborg's opinion, is very substantial. He added:

> Only as he gets good "passing grades" in these areas can he hope to maintain the company's legitimacy; and without that, the company is ultimately headed for costly, if not fatal, trouble. So his responsibil-

ity to his directors and shareholders will be as great in this area as in production, marketing or finance.[7]

The application of this skill is made difficult for the CEO because the forces pressing their demands on the corporation are constantly changing. Ruben F. Mettler, the CEO of TRW, said in a lecture at Purdue University in 1976:

> The point of balance between the needs and interests of corporate constituents will change with time and with political, economic, and social trends. The values of the top management of a corporation, and of its constituents, will also change. This means that goals and strategies must be continually reexamined or modified, as the environment changes both inside and outside the corporation. The willingness and capacity to adapt to meet these changing conditions becomes a barometer of success for the corporation.[8]

It is readily apparent that balancing constituent interests involves for the CEO balancing a wide range of economic, political, social, and judicial considerations. It would seem that CEOs faced with decision-making in this area would be concerned about the contradictions between competing forces. To test this, we presented the following comment by Courtney C. Brown (former Dean, Graduate School of Business, Columbia University) to a number of CEOs and asked for their comment:

> The central issue is the urgent need to find, within the purposes, administrative structures, and functioning of the corporation, a workable reconciliation between two powerful and contradictory sets of social values: humanism and materialism, the whole man and economic man. The social values of compassion, collective group action, collaboration, consensus, and conservation are now challenging the antithetical values on which the corporation has for two or more centuries built its great strength: the natural laws of science, individualism and self-reliance, the rewards and penalties of competition, authority based on hierarchy, and the aggressive exploitation of nature.[9]

This is certainly a perceptive analysis of the situation of the business corporation today, but it is not couched in the terms that the sample CEOs saw things. Not one CEO said he felt any strong contradiction in decision-making as a result of the forces pressing on him, *so defined*. Does this indicate that they are not really balancing the many interests focused on the enterprise and are subordinating noneconomic to economic interests? We do not think so. Indeed, the companies represented in this study have contributed in many ways to a large number of social programs. Rather these CEOs don't formulate the issues at such a philosophical level.

The CEOs in this sample accepted the need to balance legitimate constituent interests as part of their managerial job. While difficult, the balancing task is not perceived as embodying overwhelming contradictions. Donald Seibert had this to say about it:

> No, I can't say that I experience conflict. I think that there are problems, but I don't want to portray them as representing conflict because very often the various goals and ends come together. From the very founding of our company we have focused equally on corporate results and on our responsibility to the people who help create the profits, the customers that we serve, and the communities in which we do business. We try to make a fair profit, but not all the profit the traffic will bear.
>
> We put a lot of emphasis on, and we appraise people for, their community relations. We want our managers to be involved in the United Way, the hospital fund drive, and other community activities. We run our own recognition program for people who have done useful and unusual things in their communities. In this city (New York), we've run remedial courses for some of our high school graduates in order to bring them up to a level necessary to qualify for jobs in this company. We have programs to provide work for inner-city people.
>
> I don't view all of this as being purely humanitarian because, if you look at the total community, you end up saying to yourself that you can't have a healthy business in a sick community. All these activities —and there are many more examples of people in our company contributing to their communities—have had a very positive effect on our people. People can be proud of their company, or they can just go to work. To the extent that you can express the company's pride in what they are doing in these areas they perform much better.[10]

There has also been a willingness, on occasion, to sacrifice short-range economic interests. As William S. Sneath said:

> Sometimes there is good reason to sacrifice efficiency in the name of social justice and other quality-of-life goals that have become increasingly important to most Americans.[11]

To the CEOs, there were more important puzzles in the balancing act than the conflict among the various claimants. For example: precisely what are the legitimate demands of the constituents of our company? Exactly what are—and should be—the obligations of the company with respect to them? Just what response is appropriate? How can we best organize to implement the response? These are very difficult questions to answer. Later we will review how the larger companies in particular have made important internal organizational and decision-making changes to help CEOs grapple with these problems.

Responsibility for Advocacy

Sixth, the CEO must assume a personal responsibility for effective advocacy, activism, and outspokenness on behalf of his company.

The motivations for becoming involved in the public forum were discussed previously. Our attention here is focused on what generally is meant when CEOs speak of the needed capabilities to be effective in this area. B. F. Biaggini, Chairman, Southern Pacific Company, sketches the scope of this responsibility in these words:

> We have hundreds of trade associations, taxpayers' groups and company legislative advocates operating at all levels of government. We must give them strong support and help to raise their competency in all the good things they are doing. At the same time we must recognize that it's a new ball game in the government relations field today, which in many cases calls for the personal involvement of the chief executive officer. It's important that he delegate some of his more traditional assignments and clear the time to communicate directly and consistently with Washington and Sacramento on some of the priority items that can make or break our businesses. It's that kind of steady representation from the top which will build credibility for our companies with their government . . . we must go out and *be* spokesmen. Accept the service club speaking dates as always, but do more than talk to those who are already converts. Appear on the TV programs. Make more time to talk to the press, and not just when there's a crisis. Develop a personal relationship with the media, promptly praising what they do well and objecting when they make serious errors. Testify at public hearings when we're needed. Go on to the college campuses and rap with the students. Support economic education on all fronts, realizing that this is both a broad and long-range effort, but give your greatest attention to projects that appear most practical and productive. Talk to the academicians, who have a fundamental belief in freedom of thought and action and should appreciate that more and more controls on business and professional activities will surely bring an end to their cherished academic freedom as well.

Talk honestly and consistently to all of your firm's closest constituencies—stockholders, employees, customers—and ask for their understanding and then their action in their own best interests. Join the hundreds of companies that have formed, as provided by law, nonpartisan political action committees aimed at encouraging good candidates who understand business' needs, and make sure that these committees give attention to varying viewpoints. United on key issues, all of these constituencies form quite an army. Think about what a powerful political force the country's 25 million stockholders could be if they were truly mobilized to support the capitalistic system in which they have such a great stake.

Strive, also, to build over-all good relations with the entire public. Only this kind of effort will regain for business a proper measure of total credibility. We can't stand by and watch minor segments of business ripping off the public and then expect their victims to be supporters of private enterprise. We have to speak up to those of our own camp who are putting the sour notes in what should be a more harmonious chorus. We have to opt for more selectivity and less short-range self-interest in deciding what our priorities should be. We have to prove that we really are on the public's side in opposing bureaucracy, and that means we can't, as a group, go on supporting high rates of government spending for just about everything the way the polls show we're still doing privately despite our public pronouncements.[12]

Mr. Biaggini is right in saying that some of this activity can be delegated by the CEO, but for more and more of it the CEO cannot delegate. Joe Alibrandi, the CEO of Whittaker Corporation, put it this way:

People are not going to listen to a hired professional speaker talk about your company. They will simply say: "There it is, there's what big money does. It goes out and buys a top entertainment personality to create an image for the company." Rather, they want to know who is running the company. In the final analysis I think the CEO has to recognize that that is a vital part of getting his job done. The CEO has to be out front. People know that he is the one who determines the main directions of the company.[13]

Thomas A. Murphy put it a bit differently in these words:

. . . the inescapable fact is that today's chief executive officer, too, must be a public figure. He must be ready to assume all of the risk and all of the difficulties that up-front visibility entails. Many of us are not comfortable in the spotlight—or on television. But, since we are intent upon developing a healthier relationship of mutual respect and

confidence with the government and the public, it is the individual—
the flesh-and-blood man who exhibits such qualities himself—who
must humanize the corporate image. Through us, the public must
see corporations in the same human terms that they see the President, George Meany, or Ralph Nader.[14]

Today, the CEO of the large corporation accepts the role of a
public figure. So far as exposure and accountability are concerned
the distinction between public officials and CEOs of large corporations has become a little less distinct. As Robert Hatfield expressed it:

> In a soon-to-be-published article a leading consultant notes that
> "People do not expect to know corporate leaders as they know their
> neighbors, but they do expect to know them as they feel they know
> political leaders, movie stars, great writers and religious leaders." Big
> business is viewed by most Americans as a faceless monolith. We
> can't expect the public to love us, but at least we can work to get
> them to know us as very real and very human beings. In order to do
> that, we must appear before them—speak out, and involve ourselves
> in all of the problems of our nation—not just the business issues.
> I believe this to be prerequisite to establishing credibility with the
> public.[15]

Of course, the CEO cannot afford and should not do all the
talking for the corporation. There should be many others in the
organization helping the CEO, picking up where he leaves off and
assuming the responsibility for communicating accepted company
policy and practice.

Ability to Communicate Effectively

Seventh, to be effective in the public forum, executives must be
good communicators. As Phillip Hawley, the CEO of Carter, Hawley, and Hale, put it:

> I think the CEO needs a great deal of sensitivity about the public
> issues of the day, and he must have the ability to formulate his or her
> thinking on the issues and to communicate it effectively. I find in-
> creasingly that our ability to communicate our point of view *effec-
> tively,* as opposed to just communicating it, makes a big difference in
> the results. Communications skills are becoming more and more im-
> portant, and that is true internally as well as externally.[16]

Certainly, before discussing issues in public, the CEO must identify those that will be addressed. He must have the intellectual skills to analyze and understand complex public issues. The issues must be reasonably clear in his mind before he articulates his views if he hopes to be persuasive in public debate and discussion. He must be articulate in unfamiliar and hostile environments. He must be able to write well. He must be able to exchange ideas over a wide range of subject matters, many of which will have small direct relation to his business.

There is not a consensus on the extent to which CEOs will come to do all of the things suggested by Mr. Biaggini. While we carried out no quantitative survey of the activities in the public forum of the members of the sample used for this study, there seemed to be no question that the great majority of them did all or almost all of the things suggested by Mr. Biaggini. There was some disagreement about the range of issues to be addressed by CEOs. Some believed that CEOs should confine their public communications to issues that directly affect the company. The great majority, however, said that they should address such issues as well as those that dealt with broader public matters, especially those relating to business generally and the business institution. This finding is in agreement with a study of the Conference Board on this subject.[17]

This does not mean that these CEOs believed that they should speak out on all subjects. Quite the contrary, they believe that it is very important to choose the subjects that they will address with special care. Furthermore, they believe that they should speak only on subjects with which they are very familiar and on which they are thoroughly prepared.

Of course, being a good communicator means much more than simply performing well on the public platform. Good communication is required throughout the managerial function. Managers must exchange ideas, facts, and opinions with other managers, staff, the board of directors, shareholders, government agencies, etc. Communication is a means of leading, administering, informing, persuading. It can be a unifying force in an organization. Managers today have more techniques for communication than ever before but using them effectively remains a difficult art. More than ever before, top executives are finding it necessary to communicate effectively with the media. Through the media business executives can have a significant influence on the thinking of the general public. Many companies are sending their managers to professionals to improve their skills in communicating with the media and through the media with the general public.[18]

Familiarity with Politics and Public Affairs

Eighth, the CEO must be able to swim in political waters with as much ease as in the traditional economic and technical environments of the corporation.

Reginald H. Jones has concluded, in a number of his speeches, that business leaders are going to have to learn to think politically in a politicized economy. He says:

> Managers of the future will of necessity have much greater political sophistication. Like it or not, government is becoming an ever more pervasive factor in economic life. It is no exaggeration to say that for most managers, the main problems—the main obstacles to achieving their business objectives—are made in Washington. . . . This is why we say that the main problem of business these days can only be solved in the arena of public policy. Therefore business managers are obliged to become students of public affairs. They must learn how to hold their own in public debate, and know their way around Washington.[19]

James W. McSwiney, the CEO of the Mead Corporation, took a strong stand on the responsibility of the CEO in political affairs in a speech in 1972:

> I question whether anyone in a major corporation should be entrusted with top executive responsibilities unless his involvement in government affairs is strong, informed and broadly based. Business—and the nation—deserve no less.[20]

Political activities can cover a very wide spectrum, from the legislative halls in Washington, D.C., to local regulatory agencies. They can range from concentrated work on major pieces of legislation to encouraging employees to register to vote. They can include participation in trade associations that in turn seek to influence public policies, conducting educational campaigns to the same end, performing services for politicians, and urging executives to serve as elected officials in communities where company plants are located.[21]

Requisite Talents for Success in Washington, D.C.

Because a number of CEOs noted that a CEO's activities in Washington, D.C., can be of much greater value to the current and future health and vitality of his enterprise than comparable efforts devoted to ordinary activities in the home office, we devote some attention here to the subject of business representation in the seat of the federal government. To be effective in the political processes in Washington, D.C., requires talents that are far different from those needed to run a business. Business managers who have sought to be influential in the political and regulatory processes have not always understood this vital point, but the CEOs in the sample for this survey do. They and their staffs, including the managers of their Washington offices, set forth in interviews with me the nature of these skills. They are as follows:

• *A good understanding of the political and decision-making processes in Washington, D.C.* To be effective in the political processes of the nation's capital, executives and their staffs need a basic understanding of how the government operates. This includes, among other things, the relationships that influence decision-making by the Congress, the President, and the regulatory agencies; the political considerations in decision-making; an understanding of the levers of power; and the composition and operations of the Congress.

• *An understanding of how politicians think and are motivated to act.* Of equal importance to a grasp of institutional arrangements in Washington, D.C., is an understanding of the way elected politicians think. The typical politician is very sensitive to the interests of people, particularly those of his or her constituents. The politician entertains the ideas of others even though they themselves may have diametrically opposed personal views, and he can freely and with good humor discuss issues with others with opposing points of view and philosophies; he understands and is skilled at identifying and weighing trade-offs, making compromises, and negotiating consensual agreements; he has great skill in sensing trends; he does not take political disagreement personally; and above all, he is extremely sensitive to making decisions that are most likely to assure winning the next election.

• *An understanding of how regulators think and are motivated to act.* Regulators generally have processes of thought and behavior characteristics different from those of politicians. However, they too are generally very sensitive to the many forces impinging on their decision-making. In old line regulatory agencies, many of which deal with a particular industry, they are generally more likely to accommodate the interests of the industries they regulate than are the regulators in newer agencies, whose authority often cuts functionally across many industries. Some have biases towards business and others do not. Most of them are persuaded by thoughtful and well-presented cases. Most take seriously the mandates of their basic statutory legislation.

• *The need for diligent homework on each case.* The "good old buddy" network no longer works in Washington. Nor is "table thumping" effective. Effectiveness in Washington requires that an executive skillfully present a well-thought-out, sensible case. This means that a case must be reasonable, contain all the relevant facts, and be presented persuasively. The homework includes thorough knowledge of the bill or regulation in question.

The presentation of a case is more persuasive if both the pros and cons are forthrightly presented. Also, the case must be presented with candor and should never deliberately mislead. The attempt to mislead often brings a quick loss of credibility. A case is the more persuasive the more the business executive understands the issues that are beyond the immediate interests of his company and to the degree that the executive reveals a comprehension of the political issues in the case. As George P. Shultz, the former Secretary of the Treasury and CEO of the Bechtel Corporation and now the Secretary of State, put it:

> While in the government, I tried to see all comers insofar as time allowed, and I found great variety among those who visited me from business. An important dimension of variability involved the homework done by the visiting businessmen. Many came in very poorly prepared, with only a bitch and a groan and without real substance to back up their points or practical suggestions for dealing with them. Diplomatic and polite though I am by nature, many of these petitioners went away feeling that I was unresponsive and unsympathetic.
>
> Increasingly, however, it seemed to me that businessmen were learning that homework pays off. This is not simply a matter of being factually informed and reasonably objective in presentation. It also means looking beyond the very narrow interests of the individual company or industry and offering some connection between what the businessman wants and the broader public interest.[22]

Roy Ash, the former Director of the Office of Management and Budget and former CEO of AMI, observed in 1979:

... I discovered while I was in Washington that businessmen who were calling on me to induce me to take this or that or some other position usually could see only their own very narrow business interest. It never seemed to occur to them to try to figure out the politics of an issue. They never seemed concerned with who was standing where and why, with what the opposing arguments were and why they were being used. Just no interest. Every time I asked a question about the politics of an issue, all they knew was the substance of it. The substance doesn't get you very far unless you're prepared to think about the politics of the issue too.[23]

Thomas Murphy summarized the current enlightened view in these words:

But if we want to have our help accepted by government, we will have to come to it with specific, constructive proposals—not as partisans, not as adversaries. *Ad hominem* arguments, which question the integrity and political ambitions of a government official, should have no place in our briefs. Neither should arguments based almost entirely on partisan ideologies or political differences. The only arguments and proposals we should even consider taking to Washington —or advancing in our public speeches—should be those that place the heaviest emphasis on the factual, scientific and legal merits of our position. Our objective, no less than government's, must be the public's interest.[24]

• *An ability to establish and use organizations at home and in Washington to help influence public policy decision-making.* In today's world of complex public policy issues, the CEO needs plenty of help in preparing a good case and making sure that it is presented persuasively. The CEO, for instance, needs to know when, where, and with what information, political activity will be most effective. He needs to know who should be seen and when, the precise nature and position of the forces seeking to influence a particular legislator or regulator, and how to build a grass roots constituent support, if appropriate, for his position. Any attempt to influence public policy is an extraordinarily complex, difficult, and demanding task, and CEOs need help if they are to be effective in this endeavor. (The nature of the types of organizations and programs that CEOs have created to help them is examined in the next section of this report.)

• *A sensitivity to and understanding of public opinion and how to influence it.* Abraham Lincoln more than a century ago showed keen appreciation for public opinion when, as a candidate for the U.S. Senate, he said in a campaign speech in Ottawa, Illinois:

In this and like communities, public sentiment is everything. With public sentiment, nothing can fail; without it nothing can succeed. Consequently he who moulds public sentiment goes deeper than he who enacts statutes or pronounces decisions. He makes statutes and decisions possible or impossible to be executed.

Today's CEO understands the power of public opinion. He is sensitive to it and seeks appropriate ways to influence it. Few, if any, however, are satisfied with their knowledge and capability in this area.

• *Recognizing and understanding from many lessons of experience what not to do.* Many executives mentioned numerous pitfalls that should be avoided if one is to be effective in Washington. Illustrative of the "don'ts" that were mentioned are the following:

> Don't be too demanding.
> Don't assume that because a senator or congressman agreed to do something over the telephone that you have that vote.
> Don't be vague about what you want.
> Don't cover too many issues at one time. Be selective.
> Don't come to Washington too often. Don't overexpose, but avoid one-night stands. Continuous but selective contact is preferred.
> Don't "preach" to legislators or regulators.
> Don't assume that the CEO is the only person from the company who can be effective in a particular situation.
> Conversely, don't assume that staff can do what in fact only the presence of the CEO can do.
> Don't be shy about seeking to influence public policy.

There are some who hold that business effort to influence public policy is wrong in principle. This attitude is quite inappropriate; CEOs, like any other citizen, have every right to petition government. Henry Ford II many years ago put the right perspective on this point:

> There is a widespread misconception that it is somehow wrong for corporations thus to attempt to influence legislation affecting their interests. Nothing could be further from the truth. . . . The problem with "lobbying" activities is not to conceal their existence, nor to apologize for them, but to make sure they are adequate, effective and impeccably correct in conduct.[25]

• *A recognition of dangers in becoming involved in political processes.* CEOs generally recognize the many risks associated with involvement in the processes of government, but those in this sample believed the advantages of involvement well outweighed the risks. To illustrate some of the risks, an executive may be misquoted, or quoted out of context, with adverse effects on him personally or on the company. He may be treated rudely in testifying before Congress. Those on the opposite side of an issue may accuse the CEO of all sorts of postures, interests, and activities that are alleged to be contrary to the public interest. Even associates, shareholders, and customers may not agree with the CEO's position and tell him so in strong language. Still the advantages are worth the risks in the opinion of our sample.

Strategic Imagination for the Future

Ninth, the CEO is becoming more of a strategist than his predecessors. As David Rockefeller put it:

> Anticipating and planning for constant change will be a key responsibility of the top manager. Contingency planning will become more important. By contrast, CEO decision-making on matters of day-to-day performance will become less critical and increasingly delegated. In its place, the Chief executive will be expected to provide the *vision,* state the *mission* and set the *tone* for his organization's future.[26]

In other words, the CEO must today spend relatively more time on strategic matters and cannot devote as much time to tactical administrative affairs as in the past.

Tenth, the CEO must have a more global perspective than in the past. Both CEOs of multinational corporations as well as those with companies doing business only in the United States must be increasingly sensitive and appropriately responsive to what is going on in other parts of the world as it becomes more and more complex and interrelated. Today, a producer of athletic equipment, a chicken farmer, or a producer of special high technology can go bankrupt or face serious cash flow problems because of a move by a foreign country that is suddenly opposed by the United States government. What happens in so many parts of the world is now so significant to companies that those that might be vulnerable to potential adverse impacts must maintain a careful surveillance of these areas and forces. CEOs feel the need today to have an understanding of the political and social, as well as the economic changes that are taking place abroad as well as at home. Only with global intelligence can decision-making be global, that is, movements of capital and products can be made where the cost is least but modified as social and political factors dictate.

Eleventh, the CEO must have a broad-gauged intellect. As David Rockefeller put it:

> To deal with the delicate and divergent internal and external forces of the day, the top manager will have to be a "generalist," in the very best sense of the word—with a feel for history, politics, literature, current events and the arts; in addition to being a highly qualified professional manager. He will have to be sensitive to public opinion and respectful of the fragile public franchise over which he presides.
>
> The changing attitudes and aspirations of his work-force will require increased human relations skills—to deal with the growing pressures for job enlargement, more flexible scheduling, more equality of opportunity, and a greater voice in corporate decision-making.[27]

Franklin Murphy expressed this attribute in these words:

> The person who succeeds me has got to be someone who is thoughtful, someone who reads, someone who has a wide breadth of interests and is willing to speculate about society: where it has been, where it is, where it's going. Only in that way, I think, will that person be in a position to measure the quality of our efforts.[28]

If the CEO is to be a skilled communicator, an articulate and persuasive spokesman for his company and the business institution, then wide-ranging intellectual interests will be an invaluable part of these talents. Top business executives must be able to think clearly about many complex issues and communicate with a wide range of people and groups. A recent study of the Conference Board concerning CEO attitudes concluded as follows:

> The number of CEOs who say they read a lot, go to lots of meetings, and engage in dialogue with others in order to hone their ideas and sharpen their wits is very impressive. But the big news is that they sound more like a group of intellectuals than the men of action of yesteryear.[29]

Set Moral Standards

Twelfth, the CEO must set a high moral tone for his company. William S. Sneath has clearly set forth this responsibility:

We at Union Carbide have had a corporate policy on business ethics for many years, and we have more recently spent a great many hours structuring a code of conduct for our international operations. Both serve well because I believe they were well thought out. But I would be the last to say our work in maintaining the ethical standards we have set is complete because our employees have seen them in writing.

It is important to see the rules in writing, but it seems to me that constraints against dishonest and unethical behavior can be institutionalized only up to a point. All who work in a corporation must also be guided by example. The examples set at the top set the moral tone for the corporation, or any large organization for that matter, and perhaps speak more clearly than any code about how the corporation sees itself, about the standards to which it adheres, and the practices it will not tolerate. Setting that moral tone is plainly the job of the chief executive and his associates. When we have made it clear by our actions and our decisions that management cares as much about the means as the ends—that it truly believes that no business decision is a good one if it is unethical—then every employee can confidently follow the dictates of his or her own conscience when ethical questions arise."[30]

In today's world, people, including government regulators, are very conscious of business activity that fails to meet public moral and ethical standards. As Mr. Sneath says, the CEOs set the standards for their companies and they know it.

Profit Consciousness

Thirteenth, the CEO must be profit conscious. All CEOs in the sample for this report reaffirmed the position that the corporation is basically an economic institution. The fundamental purpose is economic, not social or political. Its vitality and viability depend on its economic performance and its ability to protect, sustain, and improve profitability. In this light the CEO is and must be profit oriented. To sacrifice the dominance of the economic orientation would be disastrous. It would lead to too strong a social and political orientation and to the measurement of performance in social and political terms rather than in terms of the efficient use of scarce resources. If society were to lose the central focus on economic and technical efficiency of our business corporations, it would lose the vital force that has been largely responsible for the great economic advance registered in the United States up to the present time.

This thrust for economic efficiency and consequent profit does not mean any reduced attention to legitimate social and political demands on the corporation. As pointed out previously, a proper balancing of these forces can be effected by a still predominantly economic institution with the result that over time all legitimate interests focused on the corporation will be served.

Poise

Fourteenth, and finally, the CEO must maintain his poise amid a bewildering variety and range of forces in the environment and the many frustrations to be encountered in discharging the managerial tasks that must be assumed. The less poise, the less effective will likely be the managerial performance.

Concluding Observations

These are the skills that the executives interviewed for this study say are needed for the effective discharge of the responsibilities of the CEO in a large corporation. Of course, not every CEO can be expected to be unexcelled in every one of them; some companies may demand more of an executive in one area than in another, and, of course, different CEOs by reason of training and inclination will have varying expertise among these requirements. But none of the skills can be completely neglected.[31]

6

The CEO and
Line Management

DURING the past ten to fifteen years important changes in both the organization and decision-making processes of large corporations have taken place in response to the new environment in which business finds itself. New staff groups have been created and functions of older ones have been altered significantly. The types of decisions and the ways in which they are made are now significantly different. And the behavioral patterns within organizations have also changed.

The focus of our interest here is on the way in which organizational and decision-making processes have developed as a result of the impact of the environment on the management task of the CEO. We recognize, of course, that modifications in organizational and decision-making processes result from many forces so that all the changes in them that will be examined here cannot be attributed solely to alterations in the management task of the CEO. However, the main focus is on these forces.

In this chapter we will discuss how changes in these organizational and decision-making processes have affected corporate policies, and CEO relationships with line managers. (CEO relationships with staff will be treated in the next chapter.) Both discussions will deal with general characteristics of operations rather than specific details found in particular companies simply because there is, in practice, a wide variation in organizational arrangements and decision-making practices among companies.

The Board of Directors

Corporate boards of directors are becoming much more aggressive in discharging what they perceive to be their responsibilities and are working more closely with the board chairman than in the past. This new posture is the result of increasing public criticism of board behavior, which has also led to new legislation, particularly that administered by the Securities and Exchange Commission, as well as to liability suits brought by stockholders and others. It is also a reflection of the growing sensitivity to forces in the social and political environment that are related to business affairs, and the heightened responsibility of the board of directors to assure that the company is responding appropriately.[1]

Board Duties

In 1978, the Business Roundtable summarized the basic responsibilities of the board of directors of a large publicly-owned business corporation in the following way:

The first responsibility of the board is to select the chief executive officer and his or her principal management associates. A corollary function, of course, is to replace managers who do not perform to the expectations of the board.

Second, the board is accountable for the financial performance of the enterprise. It is not in a position, of course, to conduct the day-to-day operations of the company, but it is responsible for continuously checking on corporate financial results and prospects. The board should consider and act on any major commitment of corporate resources. It should consider corporate strategic plans and major strategies to be pursued by the company.

Third, "It is the board's duty to consider the overall impact of the activities of the corporation on (1) the society of which it is a part, and (2) the interests and views of groups other than those immediately identified with the corporation. This obligation arises out of the responsibility to act primarily in the interests of the share owners—particularly their long-range interests."

Finally, the board should see that policies and procedures are designed in the corporation to promote compliance with laws on a sustained and systematic basis at all levels of operating management.[2]

These are the core of board functions: providing for management succession, considering decisions and actions having potential major economic impacts, considering major social and political effects, and establishing policies and procedures for compliance with the law. Cutting across these functions are requirements to make sure that there is an appropriate flow of information to the board and that internal policies and procedures of the company are fully capable of responding to board decisions.

Not many years ago the typical board meeting dealt with operational and financial matters. Today, the territory covered is far wider and the probing is more penetrating. Philip Hawley, President and Chief Executive Officer of Carter Hawley Hale Stores, commented on this point:

> There's no question that the board today is concerned with wider issues than ever before. The board wants to know and be satisfied with the long-range direction of the company. It wants to review carefully the company's strategic plans, to be satisfied with their quality, and to approve them. It is concerned with management succession plans. It is interested in the quality of thinking that goes into the making of major decisions of the company. (There is much testing on that front.)
>
> The board wants to be satisfied that there is a management process that is orderly and works. It is very concerned about the quality of the disclosure of information, its adequacy and reliability. It gives careful attention to determining the compensation of the top executives and to the selection of new board members. The public policy committee of the board, which is a new committee, is very active in examining our approach to, opinions on, and awareness of a wide range of issues, such as contributions, employee environment, affirmative action. None of these things were part of our board process ten years ago.[3]

Board Committees

Corporate boards of directors, especially in the larger corporations, have traditionally created special committees to facilitate board activities. In the past, the main committees have been: the Executive Committee, which deals with major corporate matters between board meetings; the Finance Committee, which reviews the company's financial affairs; the Operating Committee, which monitors the company's operating performance; the Compensation and Pension Committee, which determines the compensation of senior executives and reviews pension policy and plans; the Personnel, Management Development, and Succession Committee, which deals with policy and plans in these areas; and the Audit Committee, which makes an independent assessment of the audits of the company. More recently many corporations have created a Public Policy Committee to explore the social and political issues to which the company is—or should be—responding.

All committees on boards have become much more active in recent years as a result of new legal requirements, potential legal liabilities, and a new sensitivity to environmental forces. This is especially true with respect to audit committees and committees concerned with public affairs.

Audit Committees. All large corporations and a growing number of smaller ones today have audit committees composed of outside directors. The basic function of the audit committee is to nominate the independent auditors for the company's accounting records, review and approve the scope of audit suggested by the auditors, review the auditor's report, and report the results of the audit and the committee's recommendations to the board of directors.

The typical audit committee in recent years has widened its scope of purview; it probes much deeper into the affairs of the corporation and is more and more relied on as a sort of guarantor of the fiscal and even the ethical integrity of the corporation. A recent study, published by the Conference Board, reported that:

> There can be little doubt that many of today's audit committees are exercising stronger authority than they used to. This is most easily observable in situations where, for example, there is a suspicion that improper payments or other illegal or questionable practices have occurred. The audit committee plays a primary role in finding and eliminating the problem. But any number of directors and corporate executives have stated that audit committee members have become more demanding than they used to be. They require more information and fuller cooperation from management, probe deeply if they have questions, and otherwise do business under the assumption that they have whatever authority they need to cope with their responsibilities.[4]

Public Policy Committees. The first public policy committee formed in a major corporation was at General Motors in 1970. In describ-

70

ing the purposes of this committee, the then CEO, Richard C. Gerstenberg, established a model that has been widely followed in large corporations. He said:

> The purpose of the Committee is to give matters of broad national concern a permanent and prominent place at the highest level of management—and I emphasize "at the highest level of management" —right there on the board of directors which ought to be the first to perceive change and the first to grasp the opportunity of responding to it.
>
> The Committee's mandate is to inquire into every phase of the corporation's business activities that relates to matters of public policy, and to recommend any changes it feels appropriate to management or the full board of directors. The Public Policy Committee assures us that broad national concerns are considered in the major policy decisions of the corporation.[5]

Most large, and many small, companies have followed the lead of General Motors and created public policy committees, although they have been given a variety of titles. Thus, one study of 103 such committees registered the titles, in the order of frequency, as follows: "Public Policy," "Corporate Responsibility," "Social Responsibility," "Public Responsibility," "Public Issues," "Public Affairs," "Ethics," "Public Interest," and "Corporate Ethics and Social Responsibility." Still other titles appeared less frequently.[6]

These committees typically paint on a broad canvas. Illustrative of the areas addressed are these: equal opportunity, affirmative action and recruiting practices; women in management; employee health and safety; corporate impact on environment; environmental impacts on the corporation; government regulations; corporate political activities; consumerism and consumer service; ethics; community affairs; productivity; impact of inflation on the company; social issues in countries in which the company does business; and corporate contributions.[7]

The functions of the Bank of America Public Policy Committee, for example, are as follows:

> Identify and monitor broad environmental, political, and social trends that could have a direct or indirect impact on the bank's activities and performances.
>
> Advise bank management on long-range plans and programs for keeping the bank's activities in consonance with new social requirements.

Report to the full board on the status and adequacy of the bank's overall public policy activities, with specific recommendations for improvements as necessary.[8]

The committee is composed of six members of the bank's Board of Directors and the Senior Vice President, Social Policy.

Activities of the General Motors Corporation Public Policy Committee are as follows:

It requests and receives reports and presentations from management, consults with outside experts, and makes appropriate recommendations to management and the Board. The Public Policy Committee has encouraged increasing disclosure of information to stockholders and the general public, establishing more contacts with the investment community, and strengthening and implementing policies which respond to minority, consumer, and other interests. A Public Policy Committee recommendation resulted in formation of the GM Science Advisory Committee, which advises the Corporation on research and development programs and other technological areas of business. The Committee also initiated the establishment of the European Advisory Council and the General Motors Institute Visiting Committee.[9]

The Social Responsibility Committee of Rockwell International is composed of six outside directors, and it

. . . reviews and assesses the company's policies and practices in the following areas: employee relations, with emphasis on equal employment opportunities and advancement; the protection and enhancement of the environment and energy resources; product integrity and safety; employee health and safety; and community and civic relations including programs for and contributing to health, educational, cultural, and other social institutions.[10]

The changing focus of attention and organization of boards of directors results from the same forces that are affecting the management task of the CEO. There is no doubt about the fact that these forces are altering the governance patterns of the typical board of directors and the relationships of the CEO and the board. One significant result is that more boards especially in our largest corporations are giving much more weight, in judging the performance of CEOs, to the requirements for the successful performance of the duties discussed in Chapter 4.

Corporate Policies

In recent years, more and more corporations have prepared and publicly distributed statements of their basic and fundamental aims. Many years ago these statements were predominantly, if not exclusively, economically oriented. But now, old statements are being significantly modified, and new statements are being prepared by companies that have not had them heretofore. These statements reaffirm the basic economic purposes of the enterprise but also express in no uncertain terms the commitment of management to respond appropriately to the changing social and political forces that impact on the corporation. Alcoa's "Fundamental Objectives" and "Supporting Principles," for example, are now stated in the following terms:

"Fundamental Objectives"

Aluminum Company of America, as a broadly owned multinational company, is committed to four fundamental, interdependent objectives, all of which are essential to its long-term success. The ideas behind these words have been part of Alcoa's success for many years —as has the company's intention to excel in all these objectives:

- Provide for shareholders a return superior to that available from other investments of equal risk, based on reliable long-term growth in earnings per share;
- Provide employees a rewarding and challenging employment environment with opportunity for economic and personal growth;
- Provide worldwide customers with products and services of quality;
- Direct its skills and resources to help solve the major problems of the societies and communities of which it is a part, while providing these societies with the benefits of its other fundamental objectives.

"Supporting Principles"

In achieving its fundamental objectives, Alcoa endorses these supporting principles and pledges to:

- Conduct its business in a legal and ethical manner;
- Provide leadership and support for the free market system through successfully achieving its corporate objectives, superiority in product development and production, integrity in its commercial dealings, active awareness of its role in society, and appropriate communication with all employees and the public;
- Maintain a working environment that will assure each employee the opportunity for growth, for achievement of his or her personal goals, and for contributing to the achievement of corporate goals;
- Without regard to race, color, national origin, handicap or sex, re-

THE NEW CEO

cruit, employ and develop individuals of competence and skills com-
mensurate with job requirements;

- Make a positive contribution to the quality of life of the communities
  and societies in which it operates, always mindful of its economic
  obligations, as well as the environmental and economic impact of its
  activities in these communities;
- For the well-being of all employees at all locations, maintain safe and
  healthful working conditions, conducive to job satisfaction and high
  productivity.[11]

The Bank of America expressed its social policy this way:

We recognize that we are an integral member of the communities
we serve, and that as an employer, a provider of financial services,
and a corporation, we have a significant effect on society. We also
recognize that we must act responsibly in carrying out our commit-
ments to our principal constituencies—customers, shareholders, employees, suppliers, and the general public. Since these groups
sometimes have divergent interests, the bank endeavors to implement
a coordinated program taking into consideration the legitimate needs
of each.

In addition to obeying all applicable laws and regulations, the bank
has defined four principal social responsibility goals which guide it in
setting policies and carrying out its daily operations:

- To operate an efficient business in order to provide a fair return to
  shareholders through dividends and profitable, well-planned growth;
- To deal in an honest, fair, and open-minded manner with our various
  constituencies;
- To channel our resources to fulfill legitimate needs of our consti-
  tuencies and, thereby, to promote the common good;
- To express opinions responsibly on public policy issues important to
  Bank of America and our constituencies.[12]

These two statements are very typical. Some corporate policy
statements are longer and some are shorter, but they all say much
the same thing. There is a natural dedication to shareholders and
profitability, but there is an unmistakable commitment to conducting the business in an ethical fashion and being sensitive to
social and political forces operating within the company as well as
in the company's external environment. Statements such as these
directly reflect the commitment of the CEOs and their boards of
directors. As such they are important guides for everyone in an
organization, providing a frame of reference for corporate programs and individual behavior.

The point is that the influence of the environment on the CEO's
tasks and, in general, on the role of the large modern corporation

74

necessitates a reexamination—and often a reformulation—of traditional, fundamental corporate policies if the business is to adapt appropriately. This, in turn, often requires a comprehensive restructuring of strategies throughout the organization.[13]

CEO Relationships with Line Managers

The changing managerial task of the CEO has brought modifications in his relationships with line managers throughout business organizations. While details of the changes vary tremendously among organizations, the main shifts in relationships are clear. These changes in CEO managerial tasks are of two kinds: those in the office of the CEO and those in the CEO's relationships with other line managers.

The CEO and the COO

In one way or another all of the CEOs in the sample now delegate authority that they might have kept to themselves twenty years ago, but they still retain responsibility for the operations of the entire enterprise. Some have appointed one or more vice chairmen to look to internal affairs. Many have appointed presidents whose responsibilities are heavily oriented to, but not exclusively devoted to, internal functions. Some have chief operating officers (COOs). They stressed the fact that there is no reason why the relationships between such officers and the CEO—whose activities may be heavily but not exclusively devoted to external affairs —could not and should not be completely satisfactory.

Suitable working relationships between those carrying out these two managerial tasks must be developed, and as one CEO put it, it is always a very personal arrangement. A relationship of complete confidence, trust, and mutually understood communication must be developed. It means that each officer must fully understand what the other is doing and why. There must be a viable working relationship. It must be, simply, a normal working relationship between two people who can easily work together. The executives in this sample seemed to be quite comfortable with such arrangements.

There are some observers of the business world who assert that CEOs of very large companies cannot discharge their external responsibilities effectively and at the same time deal with the details of their business as did the CEOs of the past. They suggest, therefore, that the job be divided into two parts—one officer would be responsible for outside relationships and another would be responsible for operating affairs inside the corporation.[14] Some suggest that the CEO be the executive concentrating on the outside and that the COO (Chief Operating Officer) be the one concerned with the inside. Suggested titles for the two executives vary.

The CEOs interviewed for this survey said that the CEO's job in a large corporation was indeed too large to be managed by one person. None with whom the issue was discussed, however, agreed with the "Mr. Outside, Mr. Inside" concept. They believe that a good bit of the internal management job can—and should—be delegated to another manager or managers while the CEO devotes most attention to external affairs. But they all believe that the CEO is still and should be responsible for the entire operation of the corporation.

Irving Shapiro, in taking this position, reasoned this way:

> I think it's a mistake to think that we'll ever come to the point where a man can be CEO and just be an outside person. The starting point is you must have a successful business before you do anything else. And the CEO simply has to be involved sufficiently to be sure that you've got a successful operation.[15]

The CEOs believe that a split in overall responsibility for a company would be a mistake because the chief operating officer would be insulated from public reality, public pressures, and public conventions. And they fear that insulating the CEO from the internal decision making of the company would seriously erode the creditability of that executive both internally and externally.

Richard R. Shinn, the CEO of the Metropolitan Life Insurance Company, put it this way:

> The chairman and the president must work very closely with one another. The idea of having them in two separate worlds is wrong. Of course, each of them must have his own responsibilities. But I think the president must get outside his office; otherwise he could well become ingrained with only internal affairs. On the other hand, the chairman must be informed of some of the nitty-gritty problems of the company.[16]

CEO Relationships with Other Line Managers

Important changes have taken place in the relationships between the CEO and other line managers as a result of the changing managerial tasks of the CEO. Noteworthy has been the recentralization of authority over certain environmental affairs at the same time that there has been the additional delegation of authority over other external affairs. Virtually all—if not all—in the sample of companies for this study have programs to sensitize managers to the changing environment. These programs will be listed later. Finally, rewards systems are changing to recognize new responsibilities of managers in dealing with external affairs.

Not all changes in CEO-line manager relationships are directly connected to the impact of the environment on the CEO's tasks, but the link is sufficiently strong to examine it here. Of course, there are other changes taking place in the relationships of CEOs with their line managers, but they are beyond the limits of this report.

Centralization and Decentralization. As a result of the rapid growth of regulations concerning environmental, consumer, product, and workplace affairs, together with difficult problems in implementing the regulations, large companies have centralized direction over such matters in one or more departments located at central headquarters. In the early development of these regulations, in the mid-1960s for instance, many companies relied on their individual operating units to do what was required. There was not a need in most companies for much corporate level supervision. As the number of regulations mounted, became more difficult to understand, involved more and more complex legal, technical, economic, and administrative problems in implementation, and required new and massive reporting, the need for centralization of policy, implementation surveillance, and reporting to government agencies became more apparent in more companies. The result, of course, was a withdrawal of managerial authority that heretofore had been lodged in operating divisions.

At the same time, authority concerning external affairs has been decentralized. CEOs do not believe that they alone are responsible for interfacing with the external social and political environment. They believe that dealing with this environment is a responsibility that is shared with their line managers and other employees of the enterprise.

Sensitizing Managers to the Changing Environment. All CEOs to whom the issue was addressed believe that it is very important that managers, and employees, throughout the organization become more sensitized to the changing social and political environment and to the effects of these changes within the company. This was high on the agenda of most companies because CEOs believe that the more attuned the managers, staff, and employees are to the changing environment the easier the CEO's task in adapting appropriately to that environment will be. Furthermore, they believe that more informed people make better decisions. The better informed people in organizations are, the more able will they be to handle external and internal relations most effectively.

Franklin Murphy made the case for sensitizing managers throughout an organization this way:

> Take our forest products operations. If we put a manager in that division who tells the environmentalists that he won't talk with them because they are creating nothing but problems for him, that he knows how to turn out newsprint at the lowest possible cost, and that is what he is supposed to do, he's going to be a disaster. He's got to know how to turn out newsprint, but he's also got to be the link between the corporation and the broader real world—not the world he would like to have it be.[17]

In most companies, there is a good bit of communication among division managers, headquarter staffs, and top management about dealing with environmental forces affecting the company. The process is influenced, of course, by management style, company organization, the type of environmental forces having the most impact on the company, and so on.

Fred O'Green, the CEO of Litton Industries, explains how he stimulates his managers in regular management meetings to be appropriately concerned with external forces:

> I think that all of our managers right down the line have got to be aware of the external forces that affect their divisions. We expect them to run whole businesses. Now each of them is in a different area, so they are concerned about different influences affecting their operations. And we do find that the implementation of government regulation often varies with the locale of a company's operations, so

something that might be acceptable one place will not apply else-where.

At these monthly meetings we review the operating results of each division. I share my concerns about external forces, and stimulate divisions managers to think more about dealing with them. In that process we exchange information on what is happening or likely to happen with respect to government regulations, and what the division is or should be doing about it. We cover all of the issues and forces that are affecting the division.[18]

The CEOs recognize that there is a real need to develop educational programs to make managers more sensitive to environmental forces, especially those that are social and political. To begin with, a very rough self-selection process has operated in the past that motivated people with such sensitivities into professions other than business management. Those that moved into business were taught about the supremacy of economic and technical considerations in decision-making, and their performance was measured on the basis of how effectively they improved the short-range balance sheet and profit-and-loss statements of their companies. Business mores, attitudes, and standards of conduct also were more internally centered than externally oriented. For instance, managers in the past were trained to eliminate inefficient workers and had control systems to help them to do this. Now, there is a socially perceived need to move workers into the business system who are not well trained. To do this effectively necessitates new thinking, new procedures, and new measures of performance. Finally, it may be noted that efforts by managers to become actively engaged in community affairs, whether as representatives of a business firm or as an individual, were not in the past generally rewarded by their companies. Some companies did encourage such activities, but the generally prevailing attitudes were not affirmative.

It will not be easy to change these conditions nor can it be done quickly. CEOs understand this and are experimenting with different techniques to deal with the problem. In response to a growing need, the number of programs of an educational nature among the larger companies has risen impressively. Not all of these programs, of course, are designed to sensitize people in the organization, especially managers and their staffs, to the changing environment. Some are directed towards better communication with employees, some concern better communication with shareholders, and some are designed to inform the general public about matters of concern to the company. These will be discussed in the next chapter.

Rogene Buchholz surveyed corporations regarding their educational programs that had an environmental or public policy content, and compiled the following list of subjects mentioned; the list is in descending order by the number of times each subject was mentioned:

- Internal management development programs that have environmental concerns as part of the curriculum;
- Company developed and operated continuing education programs in Washington, D.C., to teach management employees how government functions;
- Company publications or internal management monographs devoted in part or in whole to public issues of concern to the company;
- Educational programs dealing with legislative issues of concern to the company designed to stimulate grass-roots political activity;
- Attendance at outside institutes or university seminars and conferences dealing with environmental or public policy matters;
- Sending people to advanced management programs at colleges and universities where public policy material constitutes at least part of the content;
- Attendance at Brookings Institution programs and seminars in Washington, D.C., to learn about government;
- Management retreats and seminars, some of which are devoted to environmental issues where many outside speakers are utilized;
- Participation in professional societies or industry and trade associations;
- Participation in the President's Interchange Program—an exchange of executives between business and government;
- Involving employees and managers in creating social programs or in developing social policy for the company;
- Service by employees on a foundation advisory committee helping to make decisions about charitable contributions;
- Regular management meetings where public issues are discussed —these meetings become something of an educational process, particularly for new managers;
- Faculty forums where university faculty are invited to discuss public issues with younger managers for a two- or three-day period.[19]

This list should be extended to note that a number of companies have specially designed programs for executives conducted by universities, such as the "Bell (AT&T) Advanced Management Program" (one-week), conducted at the University of Illinois Champaign-Urbana campus. General Electric Company has its own campus at Crotonville, New York. Then, of course, we must not overlook organized discussions between the CEO and line managers and staff. The Koppers Company has a unique program to do this. There, Fletcher Byrom, the Chairman, personally conducts seminars for managers concerned with public policy. This educational process is reinforced with a policy of having managers assume public policy responsibilities in a fashion similar to that of Mr. Byrom. He explains it this way:

> Fundamentally the whole thrust of organizational practice in our company today is to disaggregate the corporation as rapidly as we can into complete entities where the person in charge will, in fact, have essentially the same authority as the CEO. By that we mean that they must have skill in community relations; possess a public presence, the ability to renegotiate contracts, a sense of responsibility toward the environment and affirmative action plans; and be responsible for occupational safety. You name it—these managers do it. Basically what Koppers does is to take people who have employable skills (shown by a specialty in engineering, accounting, or whatever) and assume that those who move to successful leadership in our company will be those who proceed to broaden themselves as rapidly as they can in as many other disciplines as is possible—and other than the one in which they have received their formal training. We believe that anyone who is not willing to proceed on this basis is not going to be a major contributor to our operations.[20]

Managerial Social Performance Appraisal and Rewards

More and more companies are appraising the performance of their managers in the social area and are using the results in determining rewards. For example, there are manager evaluations that examine how well a manager is implementing policy of the company concerned with equal opportunity, pollution, worker health and safety, community relations, relations with employees, political activity, and so on. There is no uniformity among company practices in this area except that while such considerations are a part of the managerial evaluation process the predominant standards of performance are still economic, as they should be.

Concluding Observations

This analysis is, of course, not the whole story. When outside forces affect the management task of the CEO in the fashion

81

discussed in this book—in contrast to the less complex world of only a few years ago—the entire culture of the organization is affected. This means, of course, that the changing role of the CEO will bring changes in managerial styles, communications systems and processes, ways of doing things in the organization, value systems, systems designed for decision-making, planning and control systems, new qualities and skills sought in managers and staff, managerial and staff responsibilities, and so on. Space does not permit examination of all these forces, but it is important to call attention to them here. However, because of the great changes in the relations of the CEO to his staff during recent years, the following chapter will be devoted to this subject.

7

The CEO and the Staffs

THERE is no way a CEO can keep abreast of the myriad environmental forces that he should know about without plenty of staff help. This help is needed to formulate the appropriate policies for the company in responding to these environmental forces, to devise the strategies for implementing these policies, to work out plans to implement strategies, and to exercise the needed control over the organization to make sure that corporate policies are carried out and goals achieved.

The CEO also needs much help when venturing into the public arena. He must be armed with accurate information about the political, social, and economic aspects of the issues that he chooses to address. He may want help in developing a company program to deal with public issues including the building of constituencies to support his position. Failure to do the necessary homework in the public policy area may not only look foolish, but may further erode the declining credibility of business in the popular mind.

Because of the important changes that have taken place in the internal and external environments of business, very significant changes have taken place in the functions of corporate staffs and their relationships with CEOs. The precise ways in which staff functions have changed, and the precise ways in which staff relationships with CEOs have altered, do vary from one company to another. This is so for many reasons: the style of management of the CEO, the extent of involvement of the CEO in environmental affairs, the nature of the influence of external environments on the company, the way the company is organized, and the products and markets of the company—to name a few of the more important determinants.

Since staff functions and the way in which they are organized do vary among companies, the following discussion is focused more on function than organizational boxes, although organization per se will not be neglected.

The Public Affairs Function

The current *public affairs* function is so different from the traditional *public relations* function as to make it an entirely new function. Following are the more important dimensions of this function.

The Older Public Relations Function

In a typical company in the past, the public relations function covered two subjects, namely, publicizing the products of the company and building its image. As an executive of one company explained it, ten to fifteen years ago the public relations officer put out press releases when new products or facilities were announced by management. He also would oversee advertising; if he was employed by an electric utility, he would tell people how cheap energy was and point out the advantages of *buying* a dishwasher instead of *being* a dishwasher. He would also try to offset adverse publicity. Finally, he would handle miscellaneous things such as tours of company facilities by members of the public and the educational community, and scholarship programs funded by the company. The task was fairly low-key and simple.

The public relations officer did not have much contact with the CEO. His activities were triggered by decisions of line management, and line decisions were made without advance consultation with the public relations staff. The skills required by public relations staff were comparatively simple and often oriented only to publicity.

The New Public Affairs Function

Today's public affairs function goes far beyond these boundaries in scope, substance, initiative, and relationships with the CEO. The older public relations function today is but a small part of a very much larger public affairs activity. Typically today the responsibilities of the public affairs department in a large company are:

First, to monitor the social and political environment in order to identify forces that may have a potentially significant impact on company operations. Included in this "early warning" function, for example, would be the analysis of constituent demands, the changing aspirations of people generally, changing values in society, economic changes, and new developments with a potential effect on government regulations.

Second, to coordinate the analysis of environmental forces being carried on in various divisions throughout the company. Many individuals and groups in the typical company today are surveying the evolving environment of business and their activities should be coordinated, a function that the public affairs group can well perform.

Third, to identify the forces in the environment that are most likely to have the most important influence on the company and transmit that information to top management and other staffs in the company.

Fourth, to help top management in the selection of those public policy issues on which the company will concentrate its attention.

Fifth, to prepare appropriate analyses of the public policy issues that top management chooses to address.

Sixth, to contribute to and participate in the inclusion of social and political projections in the strategic planning process.

Seventh, to develop communications programs framed within policies of the company that will be aimed at the various publics of the enterprise. Included here, for instance, would be programs to help stockholders understand the operations of the company better, to educate the general public about the company and the business system, to develop "grass roots" support for legislation of interest to the company, and to get newsworthy stories about the company in various media.

Eighth, to develop programs to advance the interests of the company in the political processes of the federal, state, and local governments. This might well include the work of a Washington,

D.C., office, which would work closely with corporate headquarters to advance the interests of the company.

Ninth, to develop programs through which the company may respond appropriately to the interests of the people in the communities in which it does business. This might include administering the philanthropic programs of the company.[1]

The Organization of the Public Affairs Function

In a large company, some of these functions may be conducted in a department other than that of public affairs. Such functions tend to fall into one or the other of two broad organizational patterns. One is a "fragmented" pattern in which those performing many of the functions report through the managers of individual functional areas, such as marketing, personnel, or finance, or report directly to the executive vice president, the president, or the CEO. The second pattern is an "integrated" one where all or most of those performing these functions report to one individual.[2]

The current trend is toward the integrated approach. The officer who is involved in these different functions is often a vice president with the title "public affairs," "public relations," "administration," "administrative services," or "corporate communications"; or the function may be combined with another function to justify a title qualified as "marketing and public affairs," or "legal counsel and public affairs." The first two titles, however, are the most frequently found. With the integrated approach, individual functions can be distributed among different staffs. In some companies, for instance, the environmental scanning function is performed by the strategic planning department. In other companies, the legal counsel is responsible for philanthropy. In still other companies, a special issues staff is responsible for advising the CEO about the public issues that the company should address. Such assignments of functions, of course, vary from company to company.

New Developments in the Public Affairs Function

Aside from the great expansion in the number of public affairs functions, a major change from the past is the almost totally new involvement of the public affairs office in the company decision-making processes. Not only is this staff in many cases now directly and intimately involved with top management decisions, but it is deeply involved with both line and staff personnel all the way from the strategic decision-making processes of the company to detailed operational matters. The public affairs function today, in sharp contrast with the past, is viewed as a necessary activity for assuring that company decisions are made with a sensitivity to environmental forces and are made in a fashion that brings the "right" environmental forces to bear on the decision.

Another difference from the traditional public relations function is the fact that the new public affairs responsibilities reflect the reality in today's large companies that economic and social forces stand roughly on an equal level with economic and technical forces in the decision-making processes. This does not mean that all these forces have equal weight in all decisions; it does mean that all are fully considered in the decision-making process.

Another obvious difference from the past is the fact that the expertise required to perform these new functions effectively is much greater. Skilled observers of social and political forces, people who understand the different publics of the company, competent public policy analysts, effective lobbyists, good communicators and writers, and those with a thorough knowledge of the way in which the company operates, all are needed. Public affairs personnel must be able to get along with top management and be able to participate in top management decision-making. And this does not, of course, exhaust the list of skills required for the most effective public affairs effort.

Public Affairs Concerns of the CEO

Several of the functions that bear heavily on the CEO's involvement in public affairs issues deserve a bit more discussion.

Environmental Scanning

Many large corporations have staff units that monitor and make forecasts about the evolving corporate environment. All relevant aspects of the internal and external environments are examined.[3] For instance, the scanning program of Sears, Roebuck includes provision for such major areas as: demographics, values and life styles, resources, technology, public attitudes, government, international affairs, and economics. Within these broad classifications are approximately 200 subcategories for which information is collected.

Generally speaking these types of comprehensive environmental scanning programs are based on heavily subjective evaluations of the environment, supported by all kinds of studies conducted by company staff as well as outside groups, literature on the subject, and interviews with those who are knowledgeable about a particular area and oriented to thinking about the future. The central focus of this activity is to identify forces in the environment that are likely to have either direct or indirect influence of some consequence on the company. They are designed to be useful to management for planning and thinking about the evolving environment. For instance, the Sears, Roebuck scanning staff unit is charged with providing information about the environment tailored to the needs of each of the following management groups: to senior officers, for overall awareness of potential external trends and events that will have an important impact on the company; to the corporate planning group, to assist in goal setting and strategic planning; to merchandise groups, to assist in their planning; to functional departments, to aid in their plans; and to staff schools, to alert the men and women who will be moving into key positions within the corporation.[4]

Key Public Issues Programs

Most large companies today, as noted above, take a serious interest in public issues.[5] Some confine themselves to issues that are of direct concern to the company, while others have expanded their coverage to include broad public issues of general importance. Of course, only a limited number of issues are selected for intensive corporate activity. Generally, only four or five issues are selected for major attention during any one year, but some companies deal with a greater number. For example, the issues chosen for extended analysis in Union Carbide's Key Issues Program for 1979 were: health, safety and environment; energy; multinational corporations and international trade; and science and technology.[6]

The key issues for intensive activity are chosen in different ways. In some companies, the CEO alone, or with the help of selected staff, will decide on which issues to concentrate. Some companies will assign the task of making recommendations to top management to a particular staff unit, such as the "Key Issues Program" in the Corporate Communications Department of Union Carbide. Some companies create an ad hoc staff task force to make recommendations. The final choice, of course, is that of the CEO.

In some companies, key issues are chosen for an all-out effort, while other issues may be identified for less intensive treatment. An all-out effort at Union Carbide would involve, for example:

> Describing and explaining the corporation's policies, practices and commitments with respect to the key issues;
>
> Describing and explaining the benefits, costs and risks associated with the issues;
>
> Demonstrating openness and candor and supplying relevant information to policy analysts in both the public and private sectors;
>
> Providing constructive, critical analyses of existing or proposed public policy; and,
>
> Where appropriate, describing alternative policies advocated by Union Carbide.[7]

An intensive program would involve the preparation of detailed position papers; the dissemination of documents to the general public, legislators, stockholders, employees; speeches by management and staff; lobbying; and, where appropriate, influencing decision-making within the company.[8] A less intensive program might involve only preparing analyses for use by a trade association.

Whether or not the CEO himself should personally participate in the company's public policy efforts is itself an interesting issue of corporate policy and strategy. The Conference Board made a survey of CEO attitudes about the appropriate degree of public CEO involvement in public policy matters and came to some conclusions of relevance here. Among other things, the CEOs were asked the following questions. The proportion responding affirmatively is indicated after each question.

1. Do you feel you should personally and actively express your views on public policy issues at senior government levels? (2.4 percent said yes.)

2. Do you feel that you should make your views on major public issues known to your direct constituencies? (21.9 percent said yes.)

3. Do you feel that you should "take your views to the people?" (27.8 percent said yes.)

4. Do you feel you should take an active and public role in politics? (41.4 percent answered yes.)
5. Do you feel that you should take time out for public service on a full-time basis? (6.4 percent answered yes.)[9]

This survey did not claim to represent the thinking of all CEOs in the United States since only 17 percent of the 2,735 question-naires sent were returned. It is, however, probably a good reflection of their views. (Since the CEOs sampled for our study were not queried on these subjects, their collective answers are not known. It is a good guess, however, that most of them would respond affirmatively to questions #2, #3, and #4.)

In another question of the Conference Board survey, about 75 percent of the CEOs thought that they should speak out on matters affecting the broader public interest while 25 percent said that they should not do so but rather stick to company-related issues. For most of the latter it seems that concern for broad policy issues is of lesser importance than running the company.[10] (Here again, views of the CEOs interviewed in the present study were not tabulated, but if they were we would expect that the majority would fall into the first category—favoring involvement in public policy issues dealing with matters broader in scope than their own companies.)

Public Policy Research

Some companies maintain small staffs of highly qualified personnel, often with Ph.D. degrees, to engage continually in research associated with public policies. General Electric's Public Policy Research staff, for instance, is required to provide studies on policy issues and social/political/economic questions for use in policy formulation and strategy planning; to provide analyses for the CEO in his role as business spokesman on national public policy issues; to provide analyses on policy issues for other corporate staff in discharging their responsibilities; to maintain liaison with researchers in the academic world, and in other research and professional organizations, and to encourage research in other organizations in selected policy areas. At General Electric, as well as in other companies, ad hoc groups are often formed to deal with particular public policy issues.

Corporate Social Policy Committee

A number of companies have corporate social policy committees in addition to board public policy committees and key issues programs. Where such multiple committees exist in the same broad area they obviously must be carefully coordinated, and the CEO must monitor both.

The description of the composition and responsibilities of the Social Policy Committee of the Bank of America will illustrate the work of such committees. This committee:

> . . . brings together the expertise of senior managers from many of the bank's operating and administrative departments, including the California and World Banking Divisions, the two largest profit centers; the Personnel, Legal, and Secretary's Departments; the Loan and Controller's Departments; and the Communications and Public Relations Departments . . .
>
> This committee identifies emerging social policy issues and considers the changing needs of groups to which the bank must be responsive—employees, consumers, shareholders, communities, and others. It sets priorities and standards for responsible action and initiates changes in bank policies, positions, and practices. It also plans specific programs to help the bank meet its social responsibilities and monitors the implementation and effectiveness of these undertakings.[11]

The Government Relations Function

As might be expected from what has been said previously, the government relations function in the typical large corporation these days is one of major significance. It involves a great many people —from the CEO down through the ranks to people in all parts of the enterprise in all parts of the country—and it involves a great many activities. A central objective of the function is to provide information to managers that will help them in devising policies and strategies as well as in determining how best to implement government regulations.

Dealing with legislators and regulators is also important. This activity is not alone concerned with influencing legislation and/or regulation to the company point of view. It involves providing information concerning the prospective effect of proposed legislation as well as the actual impacts of existing regulations. It is a function that helps to improve the quality of debate about governmental activities by introducing into it factual economic and technical considerations that are not generally known and understood. And it is positive in other ways. For example, those performing this function may work with government to develop more constructive and mutually acceptable solutions to public issues. Finally, it is positive in attempting to get employees and major constituents more directly involved in the political processes both as employees of the corporation and as citizens, who, of course, may not always have the same view of public issues as that of top corporate management.

The government relations function is organized in many different ways. In many companies, the director of government relations reports to the public affairs officer. Many large companies have a representative in Washington, D.C., and also in various state capitals. Where there is no representative in state capitals, the government relations officer in the home office takes on functions directed at influencing legislators and regulators as well as communicating with management and other staffs. In some companies, the Washington, D.C., representative reports to the CEO; in a few companies, the function is part of the legal department.[12]

Aside from the government-relations orientations of functions previously discussed, the government relations staff efforts of the large corporation tend to be focused on a Washington, D.C., office; a network of involved managers throughout the organization ("Grass Roots Program"), and the political action committee (PAC). More needs to be said about these activities.

The Washington, D.C., Office

Today about 500 corporations have offices in Washington compared with from 100 to 200 in the late 1960s. Along with this growth in numbers there has been an expansion of responsibilities. The Washington office of a large company typically performs the following functions:

First, it provides information to the company's officers and staffs. The Washington office is a "listening post" for the corporation. Its function is to monitor what is going on in Washington that might, conceivably, have an impact on the company. This encompasses proposed legislation in the Congress, proposed regulations in the

Executive Branch, hearings before the Congress, meetings throughout the city, conversations with legislators and regulators, and various relevant publications. This work comprises what may be called an intelligence gathering function. And the Washington office organizes and evaluates the information so gathered. From this, the typical Washington office is supposed to identify forces that should be dealt with by the company. The office should evaluate the probabilities of actions and make recommendations about dealing with them in Washington or elsewhere.

In general, a company's office in Washington, D.C., sends out a steady flow of information about political, economic, and regulatory matters to company officers and staff throughout the company. The Washington office is the center of a communications system that can include a range of channels running from a daily newsletter to telephone conversations. Some Washington representatives make periodic visits to company headquarters to give prepared talks to various groups from the board of directors to seminars of corporate managers and staff personnel.

Second, the Washington, D.C., office provides service for visiting personnel from the company. This is a very important and demanding responsibility. For the CEO, for instance, it may mean that the Washington office will make preliminary visits and phone calls to key people in Washington to help determine who the CEO should see and when, and what should be done to prepare for the visit. Such decisions are made on the basis of the Washington staff's continual knowledge of the thinking of key people in the capital, its working relationships with them and their staffs, and its substantive knowledge of the issues involved. The better this work is performed, of course, the less the CEO will have to do and the more effective his efforts will be.

In a similar fashion, but in different degrees depending on the subject, the Washington office may work with visiting technical people from the company. Such personnel may visit Washington for many reasons: to testify before the Congress, to seek clarification or modification of proposed or actual regulations, to prepare a working relationship with a government agency, which may be a customer of the company, or to resolve a dispute between the company and a government agency.

Third, the company's office in Washington, D.C., represents the company among various agencies in the Executive Branch and among members of the Congress. This is a lobbying function in which the Washington representative presents the company's point of view as an important influence in the decision-making concerning a particular issue. This is not an invidious function as some people believe. It can be very helpful to a legislator or regulator in explaining the potential consequences of some action, which the government official wants to know about. It can serve the purpose of presenting to the government official an alternative constructive proposal designed to achieve a purpose that the company considers to be in the public interest. It can, and often is, an effort to prevent the passage of a piece of legislation or regulation that the company rejects. In addition to lobbying, the Washington office sometimes directly represents the company in various business matters involving government agencies. This can be an important role since many companies do a considerable amount of business with government agencies.

Fourth, the Washington office provides analysis and research. Some Washington offices prepare briefing papers for home office consumption or for use in face-to-face meetings of company officials and government officials. These meetings can range from testimony before committees of the Congress to informal presentations to a government official. The subject matter may range from a recommendation to the company for a change in strategy to an analysis of the technical consequences of a proposed new regulation.

In a different area, the Washington office may analyze possible new markets for company products or new government proposals for new products. The latter function is particularly important to the aerospace companies. Such analysis may be made by staff of the Washington office or in cooperation with the home marketing staff.

Fifth, the Washington office must coordinate its activities with many other organizations in Washington and elsewhere. For example, it must coordinate its activities with business organizations such as the Chamber of Commerce as well as with trade associations.

Sixth, it is important that this office have a thorough knowledge of what is going on in the company that may affect decision-making in Washington, which, in turn, may subsequently affect the company. This includes an activity that is likely to initiate an undesirable government action, or it may involve matching a new government product need with the capability of the company to produce the product.

Finally, the work of the Washington office can be done more effectively if its staff knows and understands the thinking of the people in Washington and in the company who are or will be important in the decision-making processes. This means, of course, continual association in one way or another with these people.

It should be noted that corporate representation in state capitals is also growing. It is not nearly as extensive as that in Washington, but the thrust is for representatives at state capitals to take on the type of functioning described here.

Grass Roots Programs

It soon became apparent, once executives decided to become deeply involved in the political processes, that various constituents of companies who had interests similar to that of management could be valuable allies in the halls of government. Legislators must be elected and they are known to be particularly sensitive to the voices of their constituents. Many business executives have heard legislators say:

> I agree with your point of view, but I don't get any sense that anybody in my district or my state agrees with you. I am the representative of my constituents, and, therefore, in the final analysis I can't vote for you on this issue.

Since many of the constituents in a Congressional district, for instance, have jobs with a company or in other ways find their well-being tied directly to that company's strength and vitality, they constitute a natural source of support for much of the company's business point of view in the political processes.

There are millions of constituents of the corporation who are potential allies. They include employees, stockholders, people in communities where plants are located, retirees, labor unions, suppliers, and customers. The interests of people in these publics do not always coincide (congruity of interest declines as one goes down this list), but many times they do. It is the function of the public affairs division of a corporation to determine when they do and how their support can be elicited. These efforts are grass roots programs.

A recent survey of 211 companies by the Conference Board revealed that 54 percent have grass roots programs. While there were a few programs introduced as far back as 1940, the great bulk of them were formed after 1975.[13]

Grass roots programs seek to give business a proper role in influencing public decisions, but the fundamental purposes of such programs are not solely to serve the self-interests of the top management of the corporations of this country, as some critics allege. For example, T. S. Thompson, Vice President Corporate Affairs for the Continental Group. stated in launching that company's grass roots program:

> ... Continental . . . has been pursuing a path of constructive involvement with our Federal Government. In this Washington involvement we have come to better understand the governmental process, the democratic process upon which government is based and the vital role that "advocates" play in the process. The impact of these advocates is quite evident when one considers the consumer movement, the environmental movement and certainly the labor movement, and the dramatic changes these movements have brought about in our country. But what has been missing far too long is a positive advocacy for business. This voice for business need not be in opposition to that of other advocates, but would keep government informed of the role of business in our American economy and in our free society. Government people need to know what effect proposed legislation or regulation will have upon business and upon the millions of Americans who earn their living at work in American business today.
>
> The purpose, then, for understanding our Public Affairs Program is to achieve and coordinate an ongoing local involvement of Continental people in our Government Relations activity in Washington. Our goal is to provide informed and constructive input to the process of government to enable those who have the responsibility of governing to better understand the impact of legislation and regulation on business in general and Continental in particular. Our positions on these issues will always be taken with the health of our American economy and our free society as the overriding objective.[14]

Different corporate grass roots programs operate in different ways, but basically they are efforts to organize the personnel of a company throughout its plants to help the company make its point of view heard in the seats of government; to stimulate employees to monitor, be sensitive to, and communicate to company executives information about impending or proposed government actions that will be of interest to the company; and to stimulate employees to become politically involved generally. No employee is forced to be involved in such grass roots activities where his point of view differs from that of the corporation.

Corporate grass roots programs require first of all the selection of a range of representatives with different skills who can perform a variety of functions. A representative might be a plant manager or some other person in each of the plants of the company. He or she might be a sales manager, a public affairs officer, or someone who is active in political affairs and knows local representatives either in Washington or in the state capital.

Once the company's representatives have been identified, programs are begun to provide them with information that will be useful in their presentation of the company's point of view. The responsibilities of these grass roots representatives will include developing working relationships with government officials at the federal, state, and local levels, participating in various community activities, responding to requests for political involvement made by the corporate public affairs or government regulation officers, and monitoring and reporting government or community activities that may have an impact on the company.

If the body of representatives is not too large, they may meet in Washington for seminars at which the Washington office staff and others explain the decision-making processes in Washington, pending legislation that may be of interest to the company, and similar matters. If the body of representatives is large, the Washington office staff and others may visit company representatives singly or in groups to convey the same type of information.

Companies often prepare manuals for their grass roots representatives. These may include such topics as explanations of the legislative processes; a copy of lobbying laws; company position papers on key issues; names, addresses, and background information about local legislators; the size of the company's local payroll; how many people are employed in the local area; how much in taxes the company pays; and so on.[15] Representatives are kept informed by various channels of communications such as periodic newsletters, occasional position papers on specific issues, seminars, letters from headquarters, and so on.

Many companies instruct representatives about the protocol of writing personal letters to government representatives such as how to address them, how to avoid jargon, when to write them, and other information about making letters persuasive. The goal is to show representatives how to prepare letters that are likely to be taken seriously by government officials. It is hoped, of course, that representatives will be active in developing personal relationships with government officials, community leaders, and others so that when the occasion arises they can ask for help in presenting the company point of view.

How much time and effort a representative will devote to such a program will depend, of course, on the representative. Generally, corporations try not to ask too much. The usual practice is to activate the network to concentrate on a particular issue about half a dozen, or less, times a year. When called on, the representative is supposed to organize help from constituents and key leaders in a community to write letters and in other ways communicate to government officials their concern about the issue, which, presumably, is similar to that of the company.

Political Action Committees

Corporations were permitted to establish so-called political action committees (PACs) by an advisory ruling of the Federal Election Campaign Committee in 1975. That ruling was endorsed by the Congress in amendments in 1976 to the Federal Election Campaign Act of 1974. Corporations at first were very slow to create and use PACs, but the pace of development accelerated in 1977–78 and then slowed down.

Corporations were cautious in developing PACs in 1975 and 1976 for fear of being accused of manipulating politicians with slush funds, and of coercing employees to contribute. Furthermore, there was uncertainty about a few sections of the law. For example, one section seemed to say that corporations doing business with the government could not contribute to political parties. This was cleared up later and these companies clearly can do so.

A PAC can solicit funds from individuals and distribute them to candidates for public office and to political parties. Companies cannot, of course, coerce contributions, and they are very careful to avoid any appearance of doing so. PACs may contribute no more than $5,000 per election to candidates and their committees, $20,000 per calendar year to national political party committees, and $5,000 per year to other political committees. There is no limit, however, to the amount of "independent expenditure" that they can make on behalf of candidates providing there is no request for such expenditures from candidates and the expenditures are made without their cooperation and advance knowledge.

While there is a concentration of PACs among the large corporations, fewer than half of the *Fortune* 500 companies have them.

Altogether there are a little over 2,000 PACs of all kinds. Labor unions have about 240 PACs, individual companies about 920, and all other organizations (such as the American Medical Association, the National Educational Association, farm groups, and so on) about 850. Among the PACs of individual corporations, only about 680 are active.[16] Obviously many companies have decided against operating a PAC. Some companies simply do not believe that making political contributions is a proper function of a private company. Others fear the activity will be misunderstood and that they will be accused of some type of wrongdoing or of exercising political influence contrary to the public interest. For example, the International Association of Machinists has taken the position that the employer-employee relationship is inherently coercive, and that, therefore, companies cannot avoid undue influence on employees when asking for contributions to PACs. Most companies are very careful to avoid such influence, but the union says it is bound to be present regardless of the efforts made to avoid it. The Federal Elections Commission has rejected the position of the union, and the matter is now moving through the courts. Other groups are seeking to force the disclosure of the operations of PACs as a part of Securities and Exchange Commission regulation.

The distribution of the funds of PACs is made through committees. Most committees are appointed by top management, but in some companies the employees who contribute vote for committee members. The chairmen of PACs are generally executives who head public affairs and government relations departments. Only rarely does a CEO or company president serve as chairman of the PAC committees. In some companies, as one might expect, the committee arrangement is a farce because decisions about funds allocations are made by one person. In most cases, however, decisions are made collectively by committees. Most PACs give funds to candidates that the committee believes should be supported. One company, however, gives funds only to challengers who the committee believes should be supported. This policy is based on the theory that incumbents have an advantage over challengers that should be balanced.

While the purpose of helping to elect business-oriented legislators is the dominant objective sought by companies in distributing PAC funds, there are other objectives. A study of thirty-nine PACs revealed the following stated objectives (listed in descending order of importance): promote political awareness in employees, help preserve America's free enterprise system, help achieve the company's legislative objectives, encourage employee political action at the grass roots, and help counteract the increasing regulation of business by government.[17]

Since establishing PACs, companies have reported that they have also increased their involvement in other public affairs activities. In descending order of importance, they reported inaugurating or expanding the following: employee political education programs, grass roots programs, government relations involvement of key management personnel, coverage of issues in company publications, provision of shareholder information, community relations programs, use of broadcast media, retiree information programs, customer information programs, and institutional advertising.[18]

A recent Conference Board study of almost 400 companies showed that there is a strong sentiment among them that PACs should not be an isolated activity but should be woven into its political involvement programs.[19]

Respondents to the survey of thirty-nine PACs noted above were asked where noticeable improvement had occurred in associated activities. The responses in descending order of importance were as follows: employees have exhibited greater interest in public affairs, management has become more involved in government relations, the overall public affairs program has become more effective, the grass roots political action program has become more effective, elected officials have been more accessible, and elected officials have more frequently supported the company position on legislation.[20]

At the present time, most company PACs make contributions only to candidates and parties concerned with federal offices. The reason for this is the great variations in state and local government laws concerning contributions and political activities of PACs. However, many companies have found that their employees are much more interested in participating in state and local political affairs rather than federal political matters. As a result a number of PACs have been moving toward increased activity in state and local political affairs.

Departments of Environmental Affairs

As noted previously, many companies have recently established staff departments at company headquarters to deal with the new environmental regulations of the federal, state, and local governments. They bear different titles such as: Office of Environmental Affairs, Environmental Services Department, Environmental Control Department, and Corporate Environmental Policy Staff.

These staffs are primarily responsible for developing corporate policies concerning environmental matters. They monitor legal and technical developments on environmental concerns of the company and translate regulations, laws, and various pressures from public groups into proposals for appropriate company-wide action. The staffs are usually responsible also for coordinating other corporate and operating company ideas and actions in the area, such as law, communications, employee relations, workplace safety measures, and so on. In other words, these staffs are responsible for developing a unified corporate approach to environmental policy and its implementation.

Strategic Planning

While the fundamental nature of formal strategic planning and the functioning of the effective strategic planning staff has not changed in the typical corporation, the substance has. In the strategic planning process, managers establish basic missions and aims for their companies, formulate strategies to achieve them, and prepare detailed tactical plans to implement them. These decisions are made in the light of current and future opportunities and threats, which exist in the environment of the enterprise as well as in the strengths and weaknesses of the company.

Strategic planning is a line manager function, but, in most large corporations, there are planning staffs to help managers discharge this responsibility. Both the design of the planning system and the functioning of the staffs differ from company to company.[21]

A decade or so ago strategic planning decisions were made primarily on the basis of economic and technical considerations. In more recent years, social and political forces—particularly for the large corporation—have come to stand on equal footing in the development of strategic plans. This has introduced a new dimension of major proportions into strategic planning. It has altered and complicated the decision-making process and changed the task of the planning staff.

To begin with, it is of vital importance that projections of social and political phenomena be made and considered in the decision-making process. In some companies, the planning staff prepares these forecasts. In other companies, the director of planning is the coordinator of such forecasts made by others in the company, such as public and governmental affairs officers, the Washington representative, marketing and legal staff, and managers generally.

The director of planning also functions as a catalyst in identifying issues that should be brought to the attention of top management. Sometimes, the identification of public policy issues is done through committees and/or various staff groups in the company. No matter what the path, eventually the important issues will affect strategic planning.

Finally, new skills and analytical methods are required to interject properly into traditional economic and technical decision-making the social and political dimensions that are important in developing company strategic plans. The latter forces generally are less familiar to managers than economic and technical forces. They are generally not as quantifiable or as predictable as economic and technical forces. How they should be weighted against economic and technical forces in the decision-making process is also typically a puzzling problem.

Other Staffs

The impact of environmental forces on the CEO as well as the corporation generally has brought significant changes in other staff groups, which may be noted here without any extended discussion. Many companies dealing directly with consumers have created consumer advocates within the companies. Many have named consumer ombudsmen to hear and react properly to consumer complaints. Some have hired consumer advocates from among the ranks of those who are strong critics of business simply to get that point of view recognized seriously in the company.

There is no question at all about the fact that legal departments have grown significantly in the numbers of lawyers employed and in the number of areas that must be followed legally.

Marketing departments in many companies have assumed a number of the functions, or parts of them, noted above and have, thereby, expanded their purview. These include analyzing projected changes in consumer attitudes, possible new government regulations affecting company products and services, and programs to reduce and avoid product liability suits.

Generally speaking, where the CEO is active in the public policy area he or she looks to all relevant staff functions for help where appropriate. Therefore, each department must be prepared to deal with those aspects of its discipline connected with public policy. Finance, for instance, will be obliged to develop expertise in tax policy if the CEO decides to become involved in that area. Production and manufacturing may have to become knowledgeable about productivity in the United States if the CEO gets involved in that area, and so on.

Concluding Observations

In reviewing changing staff functions and the relations between the CEO and various staff groups, several conclusions seem to stand out. First, few if any companies are completely satisfied with the systems that have evolved. Virtually all companies are still learning how best to help the CEO and adapt to the rapidly changing environment. Second, relationships between the CEO and staffs, and among the staffs, will always be in a state of flux as management styles, problems, changing environmental forces, and so on, affect the decision-making processes. Third, there is no doubt about the fact that although the fundamental decision methods are today much like those of the past, the interjection of social and political phenomena into the traditional economic and technical considerations in decision-making immensely complicates the decision processes. Fourth, line managers (including the CEO) today are now going to their staffs voluntarily for help much more often than in the past. Finally, there is no question that there have been dramatic changes in the infrastructure and decision-making processes in the typical large corporation that reflect the new impact of the environment on the CEO's managerial tasks and the growing awareness of, and sensitivity to, the total environment throughout the corporation.

8

Questions for the Future

THE conclusion is inescapable: the management task of the typical CEO of our large corporations has changed dramatically from that that was usual only a decade ago. This development, together with other new forces affecting the corporation, has significantly changed the internal line and staff functioning and decision-making processes of the corporation. These facts raise a number of important questions concerning the future:

First: *Will the external environment of business continue to be turbulent, complex, threatening, and, thereby, continue to be a concern to CEOs of the large corporation? Or will we enter a period of comparative tranquility in that environment, which will lead CEOs to concentrate more on internal corporate affairs?*

When queried about major environmental forces that are likely to affect business in the decade ahead, most executives answered that they expected the current issues discussed in Chapter 1 to continue to be problems. They see no quick solution to the problems that have a significant impact on their companies today. They see no major changes in the environmental forces that concern them and their companies. From today's perspective, it is easy to agree with this view.

It should be added, however, that there may be important *new* movements and problems in the external environment, which will affect corporations and be added to the list of those that now are of great concern to business. On the other hand, not all is bleak. There may be some developments that will be welcomed by business. In the next decade, we may manage some of our problems better than at present. A few illustrations of these points are appropriate.

We may look forward in the Reagan Administration to a slowing down of new regulatory legislation by the Congress and, it is to be hoped, a less strident implementation of current regulations. We have had an extraordinary increase in new regulations of business during the past fifteen years. The thrust has already leveled off and the leveling is likely to continue for some years unless new scandals regenerate the pressures for new legislation. This has been the pattern of past waves of new regulation. To be sure, there will be some new regulations; for example, there will no doubt be new regulations controlling toxic substance dumps.

One can also detect today a more conciliatory relationship between business and government in administering current laws. There appears to be more willingness on both sides to weigh benefits and costs. There is less acrimony in the dealings and less shrill tones in the rhetoric between the two. On the other hand, efforts to reform the regulatory processes in any revolutionary degree do not now appear to be promising.

One can expect a continuation of the growth in numbers and strength of special interest groups, and it seems unlikely that most of these groups will be more compromising in the future than at present. Demands by people to be relieved of more and more of the risks of life are likely to be received sympathetically by government officials. Instability in the world's political, social, and economic structures is sure to continue with the high probability of serious disruption from time to time.

This is just a thumbnail sketch of a few possible future developments. In pondering these possibilities, it is not difficult to argue that environmental trends in the decade ahead will very likely be even more complex, perplexing, and threatening, and that they will continue to be major concerns to CEOs of our business corporations, especially the larger ones.

Second: *Will the corporate strategy of involvement in the political processes and sensitivity to the legitimate demands of corporate constituents continue to be appropriate in the future?*

The answer to this question is clearly affirmative. The large role of government in our society gives every indication of remaining large rather than decreasing, and the pressures on government by special interest groups will likely expand rather than contract. In such a setting, the very survival of the business institution could be at stake if business managers assume a passive political posture.

Similarly, it is in the best interests of business to institute and continue a penetrating dialogue between itself and regulators about the costs and benefits of existing and proposed regulations. Better understanding between business and government about the impacts of regulation should lead to the passage of more efficient and effective laws and to their better administration. Conflicting, unjust, unnecessary, trivial, and excessively costly laws that are inefficiently administered are not in the public interest nor in the interests of business.

A recognition of, and appropriate response to, the interests of major legitimate constituents is not only an appropriate strategy but essential to the maintenance of corporate legitimacy. As Courtney C. Brown, the former Dean of the Columbia Graduate School of Business, put it:

> It is important that the corporation be preserved with its capacity for material abundance and its potential for extended public service, but in recent decades the evidence is overwhelming that it has been losing its freedom of action with alarming rapidity. The fact of the matter is that the focus of corporate purpose has necessarily come to rest on the balanced development and longevity of the corporation *per se,* and not on any one constituency, not even stockholders, although stockholders should in the long run benefit when this is more widely recognized. This is a profoundly important, but as yet not fully apprehended, shift of purposes and goals. When fully perceived inside and outside the business community, it should clarify many ambiguities associated with public attitudes toward corporations and the conceptions of business leaders about themselves. Their primary loyalty is properly to the corporation itself, and the corporate interest is best served by a balanced recognition of numerous constituencies. The essential nature of "the corporation in transition" lies in the learning experience occurring daily in corporate practice, and in the catch-up needed in corporate law, to recognize the claims of several constituencies. This constructive change is a basic requirement to the preservation of the corporation in a libertarian society.[1]

Third: *Will the typical CEO of the large corporation continue to need the skills that have been displayed by the executives in the sample used for this study?*

Certainly, the executives sampled in this study had no doubt that the skills they have used so effectively in discharging their responsibilities will continue to be required in meeting the problems of the future.

Reginald H. Jones, in a speech to the Finance Club at the Harvard Graduate School of Business, succinctly stated the requirements of the future CEO in these words:

> So the students preparing for tomorrow's leadership positions will need a much higher level of sophistication than today's managers. They will need training in the traditional skills of management, yes. ... But they will need more than the traditional skills: intellectual breadth, strategic capability, social sensitivity, political effectiveness, world-mindedness, and above all, the capacity to keep their poise in the crosscurrents of change.[2]

The qualities needed by the future CEO of a large corporation, as the participants in this study saw them, were examined earlier. As we conclude, we may summarize them by saying that the future CEO of a large company must have:

- a thorough knowledge of the economic and technical characteristics of the business;
- astute administrative skills;
- leadership abilities;
- a sensitivity to social and political forces that impact on the company;
- an ability to balance appropriately the legitimate interests of major constituents of a business;
- an ability to discharge effectively a responsibility for corporate advocacy and to be spokesman of the corporation and business as an institution;
- effective communication skills;
- an ability to swim in political waters with as much ease as in the traditional economic and technical waters;
- the skills of a high-quality strategist;
- a global perspective;
- wide intellectual interests;
- an ability and willingness to set a high moral tone for the company;
- profit consciousness; and
- an ability to maintain one's poise and composure under difficult and trying circumstances.

To this list, some people might add: "and an ability to walk on water." It is true that it will be difficult to find executives who can fulfill such a large number of demanding requirements, but they do exist in CEOs today, and it is possible for more and more CEOs to develop them. Of course, CEOs will differ. Some will have more talent in one quality than in others. But the message of the CEOs in the sample for this study is that some acceptable capability in all of these skills will be required in CEOs of our large companies in the future.

Fourth: *How rapidly will we actually see increased numbers of such widely talented CEOs?*

This question was asked of a number of the CEOs interviewed in this survey, and the general belief was that the expansion would be slow, but, in time, the standard would spread to more and more companies. Cornell Maier, CEO of Kaiser Aluminum and Chemical Corporation, explained his response this way:

> I think it's going to continue to spread. I personally think it's going to spread very slowly because we're going to need another generation of managers before we develop very many with these characteristics. I think that ten to fifteen years from now it will be unusual to find a manager who isn't involved in social and political activities as well as economic and technical affairs, especially in the larger companies. Ten years ago it would have been difficult to find a manager who was involved in social and political activities. Today we're going through a transition.[3]

Fifth: *Were the CEOs surveyed satisfied with the internal organization and decision-making processes that are designed to help them and their companies deal properly with the business environment?*

The answer is no. Perfecting organization and decision-making in a company is a difficult task that takes much time. The process of development is still going on and is likely to continue for a long time in the future. Consider some illustrations from selected areas: few if any companies are completely satisfied with their policies, procedures, practices, and results in involvement in the legislative and administrative processes of federal, state, and local governments. Companies are still experimenting with programs to sensitize managers to environmental forces especially in the social and political areas. Companies are still experimenting with programs to communicate better with constituents. Few companies are satisfied that their managerial performance appraisal and rewards system is properly geared to the new sensitivity to social forces, which managers are required to have by corporate policy.

Despite some shortcomings and dissatisfaction, there is little doubt that the infrastructure of the large organizations, managed by the executives in this sample, has changed significantly during the past decade. Policies, strategies, lines of authority, management and staff functions, and decision-making processes are much more attuned to environmental forces than ever before. But there is general agreement that there is much more to be done before the restructuring design is satisfactory to top management.

Perhaps one reason why some CEOs spend as much time as they do on environmental matters is because some concern for such matters is not widely diffused throughout the organization and institutionalized in the decision-making processes. Environmental concerns generally are not routinely handled in organizations as accepted aspects of operations. The trend is towards more institutionalization, but there is a question whether better institutionalization of the means for dealing with these problems will arrive in time to provide relief to the CEO as new environmental complexities present themselves to business.

Sixth: *Will the changes in the managerial task of CEOs and the internal organization and processes of large corporations discussed in this study be effective—especially if it spreads among smaller corporations—in preserving the best of the business institution?*

I believe the answer to this question is a clear and unequivocal "yes." I also believe that the executives in the sample for this study would agree. Irving S. Shapiro's observation is a strong affirmative response to this question. He said:

> The future role of business in society, I reiterate, will depend to a major extent on *how* business management proceeds as well as the results it achieves—*how* constructively it works with government to achieve public goals—*how* candidly it responds to inadvertent mistakes—*how* carefully it handles new safety risks—*how* wisely it introduces new technology—*how* successfully it helps to solve job and economic growth problems—*how* responsibly it blends business goals with energy and environmental priorities—*how* effectively it joins with other sectors of society to help solve our recurring national and international problems.
>
> In a very real sense, then, our future is in our own hands—as it always has been. What we do with it depends not so much on our adversaries as on our own qualities of mind and heart. If we have the will, we shall have the central answer to the future.[4]

On any significant scale the modern corporation is one of the greatest inventions of the past two hundred years. It is recognized as a superb social and economic arrangement for using scarce resources efficiently, for developing and employing new technology, and for identifying and satisfying the economic wants of society. But business' contributions to society have been broader than the purely economic ones. By virtue of its economic contributions, the business corporation has provided a basis for significant advances in the general well-being of people. It has contributed directly to this progress in providing, for example, better working conditions and opportunities for self-fulfillment within as well as outside of the workplace. This is not to deny the fact that economic progress has been made at significant social cost but rather to emphasize that the cost/benefit equation is heavily weighted on the benefit side.

Today's top executive in business, and certainly those managers in the sample of this study, operate on a much broader canvas than the purely economic one. They are concerned about their economic as well as their social and political responsibilities and opportunities. The executive of the large corporation in the years ahead certainly will not and should not neglect his company's operating efficiency and its profitability. The business institution is and clearly should remain fundamentally an economic institution. However, economic targets will be considered along with social and political programs in more and more companies.

Without a public perception that the business corporation is sensitive to and reacts appropriately to social concerns, and without a legitimate involvement in the political processes, it is difficult to envision any substantial increase in business credibility. Without it, continual encroachment of government in business affairs is inevitable.

This danger must be viewed in terms not only of the resulting loss in the economic efficiency of the business corporation but also in terms of its political consequences. Whenever the government assumes the activities of corporations operating in a relatively free market the result is loss of economic freedom in the first instance and political freedom in the long run.

The probability is high that the survival of the business institution as we know it today will be seriously at issue in the remainder of this century.[5] The conclusion seems clear that the adoption by more companies of the model of the new breed of CEO described in this study has the potential of being a major force in the effort to preserve the best of the business institution.

Finally: *Will there be a need for our schools of business/management/administration to modify their curricula to reflect the great changes taking place in the management task and in the internal operation of companies that have resulted from responding to environmental forces?*

The answer to this question is clearly affirmative. We believe that executives in the sample would agree. There seems little doubt about the fact that curricula in the great majority of schools of business/management/administration do not reflect the significant changes that have, and now are, taking place in the managerial task and in the environment of business. To catch up with these changes will require significant changes in curricula.[6]

Appendix

Corporate Officers Interviewed*

Chief Executive Officers

Dr. James G. Affleck
Chairman
American Cyanamid Company

Mr. Joseph F. Alibrandi
President & Chief Executive Officer
Whittaker Corp.

Mr. Roy L. Ash
Chairman
AM International, Inc.

Mr. Charles L. Brown
Chairman
American Telephone & Telegraph
    Co.

Mr. Fletcher L. Byrom
Chairman
Koppers Company, Inc.

Mr. Alden W. Clausen
President & Chief Executive Officer
Bank of America

Mr. Charles R. Dahl
President & Chief Executive Officer
Crown Zellerbach Corporation

Mr. Richard L. Gelb
Chairman
Bristol-Myers Company

Mr. Walter B. Gerken
Chairman and Chief Executive
Pacific Mutual Life Insurance Co.

Mr. Fred L. Hartley
Chairman, President and Chief
    Executive
Union Oil Company of California

Mr. Robert S. Hatfield
Chairman
The Continental Group, Inc.

Mr. Philip M. Hawley
President and Chief Executive
    Officer
Carter Hawley Hale Stores, Inc.

Mr. Wayne M. Hoffman
Chairman and Chief Executive
Tiger International, Inc.

Mr. Jack K. Horton
Chairman
Southern California Edison Co.

Mr. Reginald H. Jones
Chairman
General Electric Company

Mr. Richard G. Landis
Chairman
Del Monte Corp.

Mr. E. W. Littlefield
Chairman
Utah International, Inc.

Mr. Louis B. Lundborg
Chairman of the Board (Retired)
Bank of America

Mr. Cornell C. Maier
Chairman, President and Chief
    Executive
Kaiser Aluminum & Chemical Corp.

Dr. Franklin D. Murphy
Chairman of the Board
Times-Mirror Co.

*Positions as of time of interview.

113

Appendix

Mr. Fred W. O'Green
President
Litton Industries, Inc.

Mr. David Rockefeller
Chairman
Chase Manhattan Bank

Mr. Donald V. Seibert
Chairman
J. C. Penney & Co., Inc.

Mr. Richard R. Shinn
President and Chief Executive
Officer
Metropolitan Life Insurance Co.

Mr. William S. Sneath
Chairman
Union Carbide Corporation

Other Executives

Mr. Charles E. Bangert
Attorney
Randall, Bouget & Thelan

Mr. Richard Clark
Vice President & Special Assistant
to the Chairman
Pacific Gas & Electric Co.

Mr. Arthur W. Cowles
Vice President Public Affairs
Koppers Company

Mr. Robert L. Fegley
Chief Executive Director—
Communications
General Electric Company

Mr. Steve Gavin
Vice President Corporate Relations
Pacific Mutual Life Insurance Co.

Mr. Richard D. Godnow
Assistant Director
The Business Roundtable

Mr. William G. Greif
Vice President
Bristol-Myers

Mr. Emmett W. Hines
Director of Government Relations
Armstrong Cork

Mr. Robert W. Irelans
Manager Corporate Relations
Kaiser Aluminum and
Chemical Corp.

Mr. James Johnston
Director of Government Relations
General Motors Corp.

Mr. Steven Markowitz
General Manager, Government
Relations
The Continental Group, Inc.

Ms. Julia Norrell
Assistant Executive Director
Business Roundtable

Mr. John Post
Executive Director
The Business Roundtable

Mr. J. Robert Roe
Vice President Corporate
Communications
Litton Industries, Inc.

Mr. Michael P. Roudnev
Vice President Public Affairs
Del Monte Corporation

Mr. Wayne H. Smithey
Vice President of Washington
Affairs
Ford Motor Co.

Mr. Steven Stamas
Vice President Public Affairs
Exxon

Mr. Thomas S. Thompson
Vice President—Public Affairs
The Continental Group, Inc.

Mr. Jack O. Vance
Director
McKinsey & Company

Dr. Donald Watson
Manager, Public Issues Research
General Electric Company

Mr. William E. Wickert, Jr.
Manager, Federal Government
Affairs Division,
Public Affairs Department
Bethlehem Steel Corp.

Mr. Ian H. Wilson
Consultant, Public Policy Research
General Electric Company

Notes

Chapter 1

1. This section draws on George A. Steiner, "Can Business Survive Its New Environment?," which appeared in *Business*, January-February 1980, and George A. Steiner, "New Patterns in Government Regulation of Business," *MSU Business Topics*, Autumn 1978.
2. Daniel Bell, "The Revolution of Rising Entitlements," *Fortune*, April 1975. See also Joseph Nolan, "Business Beware: Early Warning Signs in the Eighties," *Public Opinion*, April/May 1981.
3. John Rawls, *A Theory of Justice* (Cambridge, Mass.: Harvard University Press, 1971).
4. "Egalitarianism: Threat to a Free Market," *Business Week*, December 1, 1975.
5. Gerald C. Cavanagh, *American Business Values in Transition* (Englewood Cliffs, N.J.: Prentice-Hall, 1976).
6. Daniel Yankelovich, *New Rules: Searching for Self-Fulfillment in a World Turned Upside Down* (New York: Random House, 1981).
7. George Cabot Lodge, "Business and the Changing Society," *Harvard Business Review*, March/April 1974; and George Cabot Lodge, *The New American Ideology* (New York: Alfred A. Knopf, 1975).
8. Committee for Economic Development, *Social Responsibilities of Business Corporations* (New York: CED, 1971), p. 16.
9. Seymour Martin Lipset and William Schneider, "How's Business? What the Public Thinks," *Public Opinion*, July/August 1978, "Opinion Roundup," *Public Opinion*, April/May 1980.
10. John F. Steiner, "Cynicism Toward Business," *University of Michigan Business Review*, September 1978.
11. Survey conducted for the Business Roundtable by the Corporate Marketing Research Section, E. I. du Pont de Nemours & Company, 1975.

12. In Albert T. Sommers, ed., "The Free Society and Planning," *The Conference Board Record* (New York: Conference Board, 1975), p. 4.
13. Everett C. Ladd, Jr., and Seymour Martin Lipset, "Professors Found to be Liberal But Not Radical," *The Chronicle of Higher Education*, January 16, 1978.
14. In Sommers, *The Free Society and Planning.*
15. Sommers.
16. *National Journal*, January 19, 1980, pp. 96–97.
17. George A. Steiner and John F. Steiner, *Business, Government, and Society*, 3rd. ed. (New York:Random House, 1980), pp. 281–82.
18. Murray L. Weidenbaum, "The High Cost of Government Regulation," *Challenge*, November-December 1979.
19. Quoted in *Time*, May 1, 1978, p. 44.
20. Murray L. Weidenbaum, "The High Cost of Government Regulation," p. 37.
21. U.S., Council on Environmental Quality, *Environmental Quality—1979* (Washington, D.C.: U.S. Government Printing Office, 1979), p. 666.
22. *1980 General Motors Public Interest Report*, p. 115.
23. Arthur Anderson & Co., *Cost of Government Regulation Study for The Business Roundtable*, March 1979.
24. U.S., Commission on Federal Paperwork, *Final Summary Report* (Washington, D.C.: U.S. Government Printing Office, 1977).
25. Irving S. Shapiro, An excerpt of remarks presented at the Southern Governor's Conference, San Antonio, Texas, August 29, 1977, found in *Across the Board*, January 1978, p. 37.
26. An interesting and informative case study of how a combination of the regulatory patterns here can affect an individual company is presented in William F. Allewelt, Jr., *Bureaucratic Intervention, Economic Efficiency, and the Free Society: An Episode* (Los Angeles: International Institute for Economic Research, May 1977).
27. Charles L. Schultze, *The Public Use of Private Interest* (Washington, D.C.: Brookings Institution, 1977).
28. James Green, *Regulatory Problems and Regulatory Reform: The Perceptions of Business* (New York: Conference Board, 1980).
29. Ronald Berenbeim, *Regulation: Its Impact on Decision Making* (New York: Conference Board, 1981), p. 7.
30. Suit filed in U.S. District Court for the District of Columbia by Sears, Roebuck & Co., on behalf of itself and all other persons similarly situated, January 24, 1979.
31. Sam Peltzman, "An Evaluation of Consumer Protection Legislation: The 1962 Drug Amendments," *Journal of Political Economy*, September-October, 1973.
32. Bernard L. Cohen, quoted in *Time*, March 13, 1978, p. 72.
33. John W. Hanley, "The Can-Do Spirit," *Newsweek*, January 7, 1979, p. 7.
34. C. Wesley Morse, "The Dow Petrochemical Project," pp. 47–61, in George A. Steiner and John F. Steiner, *Casebook for Business, Government, and Society*, 2nd ed. (New York: Random House, 1980).
35. George A. Steiner, *Government's Role in Economic Life* (New York: John Wiley & Sons, 1953).
36. George A. Steiner, *Business and Society* (New York: Random House, 1971).
37. Harold M. Williams, "Egalitarianism and Market Systems," *The Columbia Journal of World Business*, Winter 1978, p. 12.

38. Michael Wines, "Reagan's Reforms Are Full of Sound and Fury, But What Do They Signify?" *National Journal,* January 16, 1982.
39. "Complaints About Lawyers," Interview with Thomas Ehrlich, *U.S. News and World Report,* July 21, 1978, p. 44.
40. Prakash S. Sethi, "Who, Me? (Jail as an Occupational Hazard)," *The Wharton Magazine,* Summer 1978.
41. *U.S. v. Park,* 421 US 658 (1974).
42. In Harold M. Williams, "The Mood of America," Speech at World-Wide Management Meeting of the Bank of America, San Francisco, January 23, 1975.
43. David Vogel, *Lobbying the Corporation: Citizen Challenges to Business Authority* (New York: Basic Books, 1978). See also the Business Roundtable, *A Report on Corporate Constituencies* (New York, 1980).
44. Harold M. Williams, "The Mood of America," p. 9.
45. Daniel Bell, "Too Much, Too Late: Reactions to Changing Social Values," in Neil H. Jacoby, ed., *The Business-Government Relationship: A Reassessment* (Pacific Palisades, California: Goodyear Publishing Company, 1975), p. 21.
46. David Vogel, "How Business Responds to Opposition: Corporate Political Strategies During the 1970's," paper prepared for delivery at the 1979 Annual Meeting of the American Political Science Association, Washington, D.C., August 31–September 3, 1979.

Chapter 2

1. Quoted by Robert L. Fegley, "New Breed of Top Executive Takes Charge," speech delivered to the Public Relations Society of America, New Orleans, November, 1979.
2. Rogene A. Buchholz, "Business Environment/Public Policy: Corporate Executive Viewpoints and Educational Implications," mimeographed (St. Louis: Center for the Study of American Business, Washington University, December 1979).
3. Harold Steiglitz, *The Chief Executive—And His Job* (New York: Conference Board, 1969), p. 22.
4. Quoted in Norman Sklarewitz, "Pacific Lighting Corporation's Paul A. Miller," *The Executive,* January 1979, p. 9.
5. Ronald Berenbeim, *Regulation: Its Impact on Decision Making* (New York: Conference Board, 1981).
6. Donald Rumsfeld, "A Politician-Turned-Executive Surveys Both Worlds," *Fortune,* September 10, 1979, p. 94.
7. James R. Shepley, "The CEO Goes to Washington," remarks to Fortune Corporate Communications Seminar, Marco Island, Florida, March 28, 1979.
8. Interview with the author.
9. Morrell Heald, *The Social Responsibilities of Business: Company and Community, 1900–1960* (Cleveland: Press of Case Western Reserve University, 1970), p. 1.
10. Interview with the author.
11. Interview with the author.
12. Interview with the author.

13. Robert Cushman, remarks to the New England Public Relations Society, Higgins House, W.P.I., February 27, 1980.
14. Interview with the author.

Chapter 3

1. George A. Steiner and John F. Steiner, *Business, Government, and Society,* 3rd ed. (New York: Random House, 1980), chap. 7, "Criticisms and Critics of Business."
2. Quoted by Robert L. Fegley, Staff Executive-Chief Executive Officer Communications, General Electric Company, in "Acceptance Remarks, 'Public Relations Professional of the Year' " (Address to the Advisory Board of Public Relations News, Union Club, New York, September 13, 1979).
3. Shiro Ishiyama, ed., *Japan-U.S. Dialogue on Management* (Kyoto, Japan: PHP Institute, forthcoming).
4. Robert S. Hatfield, "Concerned Corporate Citizen," Address before the American Association of Collegiate Schools of Business, April 19, 1978, pp. 9–10.
5. Irving S. Shapiro, "Today's Executive: Private Steward and Public Servant," *Harvard Business Review,* March-April 1978, p. 101.
6. Quoted by Perry Pascarella, "The CEO of the Eighties," *Industry Week,* January 7, 1980, p. 77.
7. Interview with the author.
8. Richard Eells, *The Political Crisis of the Enterprise System* (New York: Macmillan, 1980), pp. xx–xxi.
9. Ishiyama, *Japan-U.S. Dialogue.*
10. Interview with the author.
11. Edmund W. Littlefield, "Critical Corporate Issues of the 1980's," Speech to Australian Institute of Directors, Melbourne, Australia, March 9, 1978.
12. Thomas A. Murphy, Remarks at Business Roundtable Annual Meeting, New York, June 13, 1979.
13. Interview with the author.
14. Reginald H. Jones, "The Legitimacy of the Business Corporation," Speech at 31st Annual Business Conference of the Graduate School of Business, Indiana University, March 31, 1977.
15. Irving S. Shapiro, "Business and Public Policy: The Process," *Harvard Business Review,* November-December 1979, p. 102.
16. Ruben F. Mettler, "Needed: A National Policy for Private Investment," *Dun's Review,* March 1980, p. 158.
17. Irving S. Shapiro, "Business and Public Policy: The Process," p. 99.
18. Interview with the author.
19. William S. Sneath, "Business and Government in the Marketplace: Is There Room for Both?," Speech before the Town Hall of California, Los Angeles, April 1, 1980.
20. Interview with the author.
21. Interview with the author.
22. William S. Sneath, "A Government for All Seasons," Remarks at the Woodlands Conference on Growth Policy, the Woodlands, Texas, October 31, 1979.

23. Robert Anderson, "Government and the Economic Process: A Multinational's View," Speech before Society of Automotive Engineers, Milwaukee, Wisconsin, September 11, 1979.
24. Irving S. Shapiro, "Business and Public Policy," p. 98.
25. Interview with the author.
26. John H. F. Hoving, "Corporate Survival in a Politicized World," Lecture prepared for the class in Business Communications, The Graduate School of Business Administration, Duke University, February 22, 1979.

Chapter 4

1. David Rockefeller, *Creative Management in Banking* (New York: McGraw-Hill, 1964), pp. 22–24.
2. Ralph J. Cordiner, *New Frontiers for Professional Managers* (New York: McGraw-Hill, 1956). Thomas J. Watson, Jr., *A Business and its Beliefs: The Ideas That Helped Build IBM* (New York: McGraw-Hill, 1963).
3. Interview with the author.
4. Interview with the author.
5. John D. deButts, "A Strategy of Accountability," in *Running the American Corporation,* ed. William R. Dill (Englewood Cliffs, N.J.: Prentice-Hall, 1978), chap. 7, pp. 140–41.
6. Quoted by Jeff Rinsgrud, "ARCO's Bradshaw: A Breed Apart From the Big Oil Chiefs," *Herald Examiner,* Los Angeles, November 4, 1979.
7. Randall Meyer, "Responding to Public Expectations of Private Institutions: A Matter of Survival," Address, University of Chicago, April 20, 1977.
8. William M. Ellinghaus, Speech at United Fund Membership Division Dinner, Bronxville, N.Y., September 12, 1979.
9. A. W. Clausen, "The Future of Our Freedom-Based Economy" (Chapter contributed for book edited by Herbert V. Prochnow and to be published by Harper and Row).
10. Irving S. Shapiro, "Corporate Governance," Lecture delivered as part of Fairless Lecture Series, Carnegie-Mellon University, Pittsburgh, Pa., October 24, 1979.
11. John D. deButts, "A Strategy of Accountability," p. 146.
12. A. W. Clausen, "The Future of Our Freedom-Based Economy."
13. James L. Ferguson, "SMR Forum: 'The Chief Executive's Responsibility for Corporate Public Service,'" *Sloan Management Review,* Fall 1978, pp. 75–76.
14. Thomas A. Murphy, "A Businessman's Concern for Freedom," Speech at National Honoree Luncheon of Beta Gamma Sigma, Las Vegas, Nevada, April 23, 1975.
15. Neil H. Jacoby, *Corporate Power and Social Responsibility* (New York: Macmillan, 1973), pp. 196–97. Italics omitted.
16. Irving S. Shapiro, "Corporate Governance."
17. *Statement on Corporate Responsibility* (New York: Business Roundtable, October 1981), p. 12.
18. *Statement on Corporate Responsibility,* p. 14.
19. James L. Ferguson, "The Chief Executive's Responsibility for Corporate Public Service," p. 76.

20. Irving S. Shapiro, "Accountability and Power . . . Whither Corporate Governance in a Free Society?" *AMA Forum*, February 1980, pp. 29–30.

Chapter 5

1. Interview with the author.
2. Interview with the author.
3. Interview with the author.
4. A. W. Clausen, Bracebridge H. Young Memorial Address, Century Plaza Hotel, Los Angeles, Cal., June 20, 1977.
5. Reginald H. Jones, "Interview," *Exchange* (Graduate School of Management, Brigham Young University, Spring/Summer 1977), pp. 1–27.
6. Richard C. Gerstenberg, Remarks at the Institutional Investors Conference, General Motors Technical Center, Warren, Michigan, February 8, 1973.
7. Shiro Ishiyama, ed., *Japan-U.S. Dialogue on Management* (Kyoto, Japan: PHP Institute, forthcoming).
8. Ruben F. Mettler, "Questions for Business Students—Corporate Evolution and Survival," Distinguished Executive Lecture, Krannert Graduate School of Management, Purdue University, August 27, 1976.
9. Courtney C. Brown, *Beyond the Bottom Line* (New York: Macmillan Publishing Co., 1979), p. 142.
10. Interview with the author.
11. William S. Sneath, Speech to Town Hall of California, Biltmore Hotel, Los Angeles, Cal., April 1, 1980.
12. B. F. Biaggini, Remarks at the Twentieth Annual Client Conference of the Business Intelligence Program of SRI International, Menlo Park, Cal., September 19, 1978.
13. Interview with the author.
14. Thomas A. Murphy, Remarks at the Business Roundtable Annual Meeting, New York, June 12, 1978.
15. Robert S. Hatfield, "Bigness: For Goodness' Sake," Address to the Annual Meeting of the Business Roundtable, New York, June 11, 1979.
16. Interview with the author.
17. David G. Moore, *Politics and the Corporate Chief Executive* (New York: Conference Board, 1980).
18. Randall Poe, "Showtime For the CEO: A TV Studio Is Not a Boardroom," *Across the Board*, December 1981.
19. Reginald H. Jones, "Preparing for a Future in Management," Speech to the Finance Club of the Harvard Graduate School of Business, Cambridge, Mass., November 2, 1978.
20. James W. McSwiney, "Let Charlie Do It?," Address to the Government Affairs Committee Workshop, American Paper Institute, Pebble Beach, Cal., August 3, 1972.
21. For a survey of executives concerned with activities such as these see Steven N. Brenner, "Business and Politics—An Update," *Harvard Business Review*, November-December 1979.
22. George P. Schultz, "Business and Public Policy: The Abrasive Interface," *Harvard Business Review*, November-December 1979, p. 93.
23. "Conversation: An Interview with Roy L. Ash," *Organizational Dynamics*, Autumn 1979, p. 67.

24. Thomas A. Murphy, Remarks at Business Roundtable Annual Meeting, New York, June 12, 1978.
25. Henry Ford II, Address delivered at the President's Conference on Public Affairs, Chamber of Commerce of the United States, Detroit, Michigan, January 5, 1961.
26. David Rockefeller, "The Chief Executive in the Year 2000," Remarks at Commonwealth Club of California, San Francisco, Cal., November 2, 1979.
27. David Rockefeller, "The Chief Executive in the Year 2000."
28. Interview with the author.
29. David G. Moore, *Politics and the Corporate Chief Executive*, p. 40.
30. William S. Sneath, "Framework for a Business Ethic," Remarks at the 22nd Southern Assembly, Biloxi, Mississippi, January 5, 1978.
31. Other lists of managerial requirements for top executives have been compiled from time to time. The latest is: Ruth Gilbert Schaeffer, *Top Management Staffing Challenges: CEO's Describe Their Needs* (New York: Conference Board, 1982).

Chapter 6

1. Courtney C. Brown, *Putting the Corporate Board to Work* (New York: Macmillan Publishing Co., 1976).
2. The Business Roundtable, *The Role and Composition of the Board of Directors of the Large Publicly Owned Corporation* (New York, January 1978).
3. Interview with the author.
4. Jeremy Bacon, *Corporate Directorship Practices: The Audit Committee* (New York: Conference Board, 1979), p. 2.
5. Richard C. Gerstenberg, "Corporate Responsiveness and Profitability," *The Conference Board Record*, (New York: Conference Board, November 1972).
6. Phyllis S. McGrath, *Corporate Directorship Practices: The Public Policy Committee* (New York: Conference Board, 1980).
7. Phyllis S. McGrath, *Corporate Directorship Practices*, and Michael L. Lovdal, Raymond A. Bauer, and Nancy H. Treverton, "Public Responsibility Committees of the Board," *Harvard Business Review*, May-June 1977.
8. Bank of America, *Community and the Bank*, 1977.
9. *1980 General Motors Public Interest Report*, General Motors Corporation, p. 58.
10. *Rockwell International Annual Report 1979*.
11. *Alcoa Policy Guidelines for Business Conduct*, March 1977.
12. Bank of America, *Community and the Bank*, 1978.
13. Melvin Anshen, *Corporate Strategies for Social Performance* (New York: Macmillan Publishing Co., 1980).
14. See, for example, Courtney C. Brown, *Putting the Corporate Board to Work*, and Courtney C. Brown, *Beyond the Bottom Line* (New York: Macmillan Publishing Co., 1979).
15. Quoted by Perry Pascarella, "The CEO of the Eighties," *Industry Week*, January 7, 1979, p. 79.

16. Interview with the author.
17. Interview with the author.
18. Interview with the author.
19. Rogene A. Buchholz, *Business Environment/Public Policy: Corporate Executive Viewpoints and Educational Implications* (Center for the Study of American Business, Washington University, St. Louis, May 1980).
20. Fletcher L. Byrom, "For the Manager—The Future is Now." *Report of the Second Colloquium: Management in the XXI Century,* A Joint Project of the American Assembly of Collegiate Schools of Business and the European Foundation for Management Development, 1979, p. 49.

Chapter 7

1. James E. Post, Edwin A. Murray, Jr., Robert B. Dickie, John F. Mahon, and Michael R. Jones, *Public Affairs Offices and Their Functions* (Boston: School of Management, Boston University, 1981).
2. See Phyllis S. McGrath, *Managing Corporate External Relations: Changing Perspectives and Responses* (New York: Conference Board, 1976).
3. James K. Brown, *This Business of Issues: Coping with the Company's Environments* (New York: Conference Board, 1979). See also Harold E. Klein and Robert E. Linneman, "The Use of Scenarios in Corporate Planning—Eight Case Histories," *Long Range Planning,* October 1981.
4. Internal communication, updated.
5. For a thorough analysis of corporate response to public issues see Francis W. Steckmest, *Corporate Performance: The Key to Public Trust* (New York: McGraw-Hill, 1982). See also James K. Brown, *Guidelines For Managing Corporate Issues Programs* (New York: Conference Board, 1981).
6. Union Carbide, *Key Public Issues,* 1979.
7. Union Carbide, *Key Public Issues,* 1979, p. 18.
8. Hugh D. Menzies, "Union Carbide Raises Its Voice," *Fortune,* September 25, 1978.
9. David G. Moore, *Politics and the Corporate Chief Executive* (New York: Conference Board, 1980), p. 9.
10. David G. Moore, *Politics and the Corporate Chief Executive,* pp. 23–34.
11. Bank of America, "Community and the Bank 1977," Bank of America, 1978.
12. One survey of 359 companies showed that 285 have government relations units. Of these companies, "94 have only a headquarters unit; 56 have only a Washington office; 104 have both a headquarters unit and a Washington office; 16 have a subunit in the general counsel's department; 7 have a headquarters unit and a subunit in the general counsel's department; 4 have a Washington office and a subunit in the general counsel's department; 4 have some 'other organizational arrangement.' " Phyllis S. McGrath, *Redefining Corporate-Federal Relations* (New York: Conference Board, 1979), p. 57.
13. Phyllis S. McGrath, *Redefining Corporate-Federal Relations,* p. 37.
14. T. S. Thompson, "Policy Statement: The Continental Group, Inc.," October 11, 1979.

15. Phyllis S. McGrath, *Redefining Corporate-Federal Relations,* pp. 38–39.
16. Public Affairs Council interview with the author.
17. Helena Elizabeth Gordon, *Corporate Political Action Committees: An Assessment of Their Role in the Public Affairs Programs of Selected Fortune 500 Companies* (Masters Thesis, Public Relations Graduate Program, American University, Washington, D.C., 1980), p. V-4.
18. Helena Elizabeth Gordon, *Corporate Political Action Committees,* pp. V-5–V-6.
19. McGrath, *Redefining Corporate-Federal Relations,* p. 50.
20. Gordon, p. V-7.
21. George A. Steiner, *Strategic Planning: What Every Manager Must Know* (New York: Free Press, 1979).

Chapter 8

1. Courtney C. Brown, *Beyond the Bottom Line* (New York: Macmillan Publishing Co., 1979), p. 14.
2. Reginald H. Jones, "Preparing for a Future in Management," Speech to the Finance Club of the Harvard Graduate School of Business, Cambridge, Mass., November 2, 1978.
3. Interview with the author.
4. Irving S. Shapiro, in Lillian W. Kay, ed., *The Future Role in Business in Society* (New York: Conference Board, 1977), p. 11.
5. Richard Eells, *The Political Crisis of the Enterprise System* (New York: Macmillan Publishing Co., 1980).
6. *The Changing Expectations of Society in the Next Thirty Years*—Windsor Castle Colloquium (St. Louis: American Assembly of Collegiate Schools of Business, 1979).

Index

About the Author

George A. Steiner, is the Harry and Elsa Kunin Professor of Business and Society, and Professor of Management, Graduate School of Management, UCLA. He has held responsible positions in the government and industry, including membership on the boards of directors of a number of companies. He has written extensively in the management field. His latest books are *Management Policy and Strategy: Text, Readings, and Cases* (with John B. Miner and Edmund Gray), *Business, Government, and Society* (with John F. Steiner), and *Strategic Planning: What Every Manager Must Know*.

ALBERT S. GLICKMAN, CLIFFORD P. HAHN, EDWIN A. FLEISHMAN, and BRENT BAXTER
Top Management Development and Succession: An Exploratory Study

NEIL H. JACOBY
Corporate Power and Social Responsibility

NEIL H. JACOBY
Multinational Oil: A Study in Industrial Dynamics

NEIL H. JACOBY, PETER NEHEMKIS, and RICHARD EELLS
Bribery and Extortion in World Business: A Study of Corporate Political Payments Abroad

JAY W. LORSCH
Product Innovation and Organization

IRA M. MILLSTEIN and SALEM M. KATSH
The Limits of Corporate Power: Existing Constraints on the Exercise of Corporate Discretion

KENNETH G. PATRICK
Perpetual Jeopardy—The Texas Gulf Sulphur Affair: A Chronicle of Achievement and Misadventure

KENNETH G. PATRICK and RICHARD EELLS
Education and the Business Dollar

IRVING PFEFFER, *editor*
The Financing of Small Business: A Current Assessment

STANLEY SALMEN
Duties of Administrators in Higher Education

GUNNAR K. SLETMO and ERNEST W. WILLIAMS, JR.
Liner Conferences in the Container Age: U.S. Policy at Sea

GEORGE A. STEINER
The New CEO

GEORGE A. STEINER
Top Management Planning

GEORGE A. STEINER and WILLIAM G. RYAN
Industrial Project Management

GEORGE A. STEINER and WARREN M. CANNON, *editors*
Multinational Corporate Planning

GUS TYLER
The Political Imperative: The Corporate Character of Unions

CLARENCE WALTON and RICHARD EELLS, *editors*
The Business System: Readings in Ideas and Concepts

The colophon for this book was created by Theodore Roszak exclusively for the use of the Program for Studies of the Modern Corporation.